Copyright © 2024 by Michelle Spiva

All rights reserved.

No portion of this book may be reproduced in any form without written permission from the publisher or author, except as permitted by U.S. copyright law.

Published by Evie Publishing
Illustrations by Sarah Parker
Design by Jason Arias

ISBN 979-8-218-41608-9

MUSIC CITY Musings

Old Nashville Knowledge for Newcomers

Michelle Spiva

Contents

Introduction — VII

Part One: Settling In
1. Am I Southern Now? — 1
2. Where to Live — 7
3. Labyrinths, Potholes, and Cranes - A Nashville Driving Story — 19
4. Rookie Mistakes to Avoid — 31

Part Two: Setting Out
5. Eat, Drink, and Be Merry, for Tomorrow We're Hungover — 39
6. The Neon Lights of Broadway — 49
7. Invasion of the Bachelorettes — 55
8. The Music Scene — 61
9. The Nashville Social Calendar — 69

Part Three: Going Native

10. Mother Nature - An Uneasy Relationship	83
11. The Pain of Being a Nashville Sports Fan	93
12. Parks and Recreation	99
13. The Nashville Way	105
14. Nashville Citizenship Test	111

Nashville Slang	121
Bibliography	131
Acknowledgments	135
About the Author	137

Introduction

According to the Nashville Area Chamber of Commerce's Research Center, approximately one hundred people move to the Nashville area every day. I've talked to some of these new residents, often while standing in line somewhere, and asked, "Why Nashville?" All the answers emphasize Nashville's reputation as being a wonderful place to live, but what is that reputation based on? There are a lot of wonderful places to live. Why are so many people drawn to move here?

I believe it's partly due to what many locals refer to as the "Nashville way." It's a unique combination of generosity and hospitality that celebrates individuality while encouraging collaboration and creativity. It makes Nashville more than just a place. It's a way of life firmly embedded in our city that's distinctive, wonderful, and, to new residents, possibly a bit bewildering.

By writing this lighthearted guide, I hope to ease your transition to Nashville so you can understand and appreciate the distinct norms, customs, and habits that define Nashville and adjust to the rhythm of life in Music City. It will help you settle in, set out, and ultimately, become a true local.

Welcome home.

PART ONE: SETTLING IN

WELCOME
TO
NASHVILLE
Does this mean we can say 'y'all' now?
NEW2TWN

CHAPTER 1

Am I Southern Now?

Many newcomers arrive in Nashville with visions of biscuits and rhinestones dancing in their heads. Which begs the question: are you Southern now?

Well, in a way.

Nashville is located at a latitude of 36.1627° N, well below the Mason-Dixon Line, but still closer to St. Louis and the border of Indiana than locals care to admit. In fact, more than half the US population resides within a day's drive of the city, owing to its centralized location.

Which is to say: we're Southern, but not that Southern. More Mid-South than "The Devil Went Down to Georgia" South.

So, how did Nashville become the incredible music city we've all come to know and love?

Blame it on an insurance company.

The Birth of a Country Music Capital

In 1925, National Life and Accident Insurance Company needed a new way to reach their customers. So, they utilized the burgeoning medium of radio to create WSM, or "We Shield Millions." Led by program director and broadcast maven George D. Hay, WSM's crown jewel was a humble radio show called *The WSM Barn Dance*, or as it would later come to be known, the *Grand Ole Opry*.

The *Grand Ole Opry* captivated listeners with its twangy tunes and lively performances of "hillbilly music." In 1943, the show moved from National Life and Accident Insurance Company's downtown office to the Ryman Auditorium. Legends like Hank Williams Sr., Patsy Cline, and Johnny Cash graced its stage, while performers like Porter Wagoner helped to popularize the bedazzled "Nudie suit." The birth of an industry would come in short order, but it set the backdrop for the Nashville we know today.

But what about everything else? There was a Nashville before then, and there is a new Nashville that has emerged in the decades since. Here is everything you need to know, in quick-hitting fashion.

An Abridged History of Nashville

There were saber-toothed cats. Long before honky-tonks or people entered the scene, prehistoric Nashville was roamed by the deadly and fearsome Smilodon. In the summer of 1971, a construction crew downtown unearthed the fossilized remains of one such cat. When our newly formed hockey team needed to come up with a name in 1997, the "Smilodons" didn't sound very intimidating, so they went with the "Predators" instead.

We legalized prostitution. During the Civil War, Nashville was controlled by Union troops, who in turn were controlled by prostitutes. Venereal diseases were rampant in the city, and in 1863 a group of one hundred sex workers were put on a boat and shipped upriver, first to Louisville and then to Cincinnati. When neither city was willing to accept them, they were shipped back down to Nashville. This led to the regulation of sex work in Nashville and gave the city the dubious distinction of being the first in the nation to legalize prostitution.

Healthcare, healthcare, healthcare. For as much of a music town as we are, we're more of a healthcare town. The city where the Hospital Corporation of America (HCA) was founded in 1968 is now home to more than 900 healthcare companies. Vanderbilt University Medical Center, HCA, Ascension Saint Thomas, and Community Health Systems are the biggest players. According to the Nashville Area Chamber of Commerce, the industry contributes an overall benefit of almost $67 billion and more than 350,000 jobs to our local economy every year. It's like we're saying, "Come for the music, and stay for an MRI."

Bill Boner and the Rise of New Nashville. In 1987, Nashville had a mayor by the name of Bill Boner who was engaged to his mistress while still married to his third wife. This mistress, a country singer by the name of Traci Peel, appeared with Boner on *The Phil Donahue Show*, where the two sang "Rocky Top," mortifying the city. Later, Peel would tell Nashville reporters that the mayor's passion "could last for up to seven hours."

After the Boner years, the city moved forward thanks to a series of competent and non philandering (well, mostly) mayors. Broadway was revitalized, we got a hit TV soap opera, and the *New York Times* and *GQ* called us "It City" and "Nowville," respectively. Cool people like Jack White and the Black Keys began to move here, as did about one hundred other people every day.

It's the American Dream, with a slight Southern drawl.

EAST NASHVILLE
How long would it take us to get over there?
Days.
WEST NASHVILLE

CHAPTER 2

Where to Live

As a new arrival, the first thing you are going to want to do is find shelter.

Nashville contains a multitude of neighborhoods, each offering its own unique flavor, community, and quirky experiences that contribute to the scintillating tapestry of the city. Choosing to rent in a new apartment complex in Midtown is going to be different from owning a home in Green Hills, which is going to be different from occupying a tall and skinny in the Nations. To say nothing of our satellite cities, some of which have their own government and police force.

To get a local's take on which area will best fit your lifestyle (and, ahem, economic means), follow this mildly subjective breakdown:

12 South: A yuppie's dream of picture-perfect streets, trendy boutiques, and upscale restaurants with a touch of Southern charm. For the perfect date night, grab drinks at 12 South Taproom, followed by ice cream at Jeni's. Cap the evening off with a stroll through Sevier Park or a little house sidewalk-shopping, gazing at the many 1950s cottages and Craftsmans that could one day be yours. Do not look up their listing prices.

- Perfect for: Young couples and families; recent college grads.
- Can I afford it?: Buy? No. Rent? Maybe.
- Alternative neighborhood: Melrose. The stench of smokers' past lives on at Melrose Billiards, but the area continues to grow and is close to Geodis Park for soccer fans.

Belle Meade: In this small town with its own police force and mayor, sitting five miles southwest of downtown Nashville, residents live in a world of their own in old-school grand estates. If Nashville had a Versailles, this would be it. The iron street signs with horses on them probably give it away.

- Perfect for: Old-money aristocrats.
- Can I afford it?: Sure, if you bought Amazon stock in the nineties.
- Alternative neighborhood: Oak Hill. Why pay

Belle Meade taxes when you can live six miles east, where the lawns are just as pristine? Bonus: you'll be neighbors with the governor.

East Nashville: This is our Brooklyn. Our Silver Lake. It's where our seasonally unemployed hipsters reside. If Nashville is the "Buckle of the Bible Belt," then East Nashville is its unzipped fly. Affectionately called "East Nasty" or "East," this bohemian enclave is a magnet for artist types with tattoos and a yen for beard oil who prefer dive bars like Mickey's and Dino's to glitzy hotspots. Locals who live in Nashville proper think a trip to East Nashville is a two-hour drive, despite the fact that it's only twenty minutes away, but the thought of crossing the Cumberland River somehow makes the journey seem like an expedition to Siberia. A lot of these locals are rethinking the journey since many of the city's best restaurants and chefs are in this bustling neighborhood.

- Perfect for: Musicians; foodies; those who don't mind the deleterious effects of gentrification.
- Can I afford it?: Ten years ago. Now you might be looking further up Gallatin Pike to . . .
- Alternative neighborhood: Madison. Or—hear us out—Dickerson Pike. Once a major thoroughfare before the construction of I-65, Dickerson Pike experienced a major decline. However, Nashville's

economic upswing is slowly transforming this cluster of pawnshops, fast-food joints, and tire resellers into a budding collection of funky vintage shops, snazzy condos, and townhouses. There's even a quirky refurbished motel with a public swim club called The Dive Motel.

Germantown/Jefferson Street: Renovated historic Victorian buildings and brick sidewalks grace this neighborhood on the National Register of Historic Places. Some of the city's best chefs call Germantown home, where the smell of freshly brewed coffee competes with the scent of ballpark hot dogs from the Nashville Sounds baseball stadium.

- Perfect for: Foodies; those who want to be close to the city but still feel like they're in a distinct neighborhood.
- Can I afford it?: You can overpay for it.
- Alternative neighborhood: Salemtown, Germantown's more subdued, further-north cousin. Or the upcoming East Bank development (we prefer "Oracleville"), which, upon completion, will be right across the river from Germantown.

Green Hills: The obvious destination for those who believe the best form of self-care is high-end retail therapy.

Sure, the traffic in this opulent area has taken years off our lives, but Nordstrom at The Mall makes it all worth it.

- Perfect for: Families.
- Can I afford it?: If you have to ask...
- Alternative neighborhood: Forest Hills. If Frank Lloyd Wright had to choose somewhere to live in Nashville, it would be here, where residents live in their private wooded wonderland.

The Gulch: Back in the early 2000s, this neighborhood didn't even exist; it was literally a railroad terminal at the bottom of a gulch. Today, it is ground zero for the new development that has happened in Nashville. So, if you want to live in a posh high-rise condo, the Gulch is your go-to concrete jungle. Here, one can find trendy stores, upscale restaurants, and the highest concentration of murals east of the Mississippi.

- Perfect for: Well-heeled city dwellers; professional athletes; former contestants of *The Bachelor*.
- Can I afford it?: If you don't mind New York City prices.
- Alternative neighborhood: Downtown. The only thing more upscale than the penthouse at Icon is the grand penthouse at the Four Seasons downtown. Price tag: only $15 million!

Midtown/West End: Higher education meets spin class aficionados in this dense pocket of newly built apartment complexes. Vanderbilt students display their unique blend of intellectual curiosity and partying ability on the Rock Block like every night is homecoming weekend.

- Perfect for: Vanderbilt undergraduates, Vanderbilt graduate students, Vanderbilt law students, Vanderbilt medical students, Vanderbilt nurses, general fans of Vanderbilt and rabid squirrels.
- Can I afford it?: Hopefully your parents can.
- Alternative neighborhood: Hillsboro Village. A little less chaotic than Midtown, Hillsboro Village offers a cozy nook of shops, homey cafés, and the wonderful Belcourt Theatre.

The Nations: Once an industrial wasteland, the Nations is now a built-up area popular with young folks, many of whom bought in early and love to tell their friends, "We told you the neighborhood would get better!" Paradoxically, the streets are named after US states rather than nations, which we assume was done to distract us from all the tall and skinnies.

- Perfect for: Young professionals who don't mind their cars getting rummaged through.
- Can I afford it?: We think so, maybe!
- Alternative neighborhood: Sylvan Park, which

lies just across Charlotte Avenue and has a slightly more neighborhood-y feel. Regardless, residents of both are primely situated to get to Neighbors and Caffé Nonna.

WeHo (Wedgewood-Houston): Artists gather to debate the meaning of a blank canvas at Soho House, and galleries showcase avant-garde sculptures made entirely of recycled chewing gum wrappers. Locals can be heard saying in hushed tones, "Mark my words. WeHo is the new Gulch."
- Perfect for: Fans of lofts.
- Can I afford it?: No.
- Alternative neighborhoods: Chestnut Hill and Woodbine, both up-and-coming gems that provide easy access to the Latin American and Kurdish culinary delights of Nolensville Pike. Bonus points for visiting Edessa Restaurant, which offers up excellent flatbreads, lamb kabobs, baklava, and black tea.

Outside Davidson County

Once one decides to venture outside the safe confines of Nashville and Davidson County, all bets are off. You're in international waters now, and we can't guarantee we'll be able to save you.

Williamson County: Families looking for more land and better public schools flock to this wealthy enclave south of Nashville. Well-to-do Brentwood makes its case for McMansion capital of the country, while Franklin is Mayberry or Pleasantville—take your pick.
- Perfect for: New-money soccer moms; people who watch too much cable news.
- Can I afford it?: Dave Ramsey can.
- Alternative neighborhoods: Leiper's Fork and Brentioch. The former is even more bucolic than Franklin, and the latter is a mix between Brentwood and Antioch, like a turducken.

Mount Juliet: This flat suburban township rises a mere 683 feet above sea level, explaining the irony of the "I Skied Mount Juliet" T-shirts (https://whynottees.com).
- Perfect for: Families, professional race car drivers.
- Can I afford it?: We think so, maybe!
- Alternative neighborhoods: Hendersonville, Old Hickory, and Hermitage. We're not entirely sure which one is which, but there's a lake up there you can enjoy.

Sidewalks to Nowhere

Whichever neighborhood you choose to call home, you might be asking yourself, "Where are the sidewalks?"

With all the construction in Nashville, the city council decided to make Nashville more walkable, but to implement that pipe dream, they required developers to pave a sidewalk in front of any newly built house. Of course, if your next-door neighbors' houses were built prior to that requirement, your sidewalk starts and ends on your property. You may have to walk two city blocks before you hit another short segment of sidewalk that goes nowhere.

Maybe a hundred years from now, all the short segments of sidewalk will link together and we'll hang a "Mission Accomplished!" banner, but probably not in your lifetime. The city council in all their wisdom has since decided to reverse the sidewalk requirement—just like they did in the mid-nineteenth century when this same story played out with residents. Rest assured, Nashville has clearly embraced the slowest method for sidewalk construction in history, taking "slow and steady" to a whole new level.

Getting to Know the Neighbors

Ann Patchett: As the owner of Parnassus Books in Green Hills, Ann is Nashville's de facto literary ambassador. Visit the bestselling author's charming bookstore and say hello to the shop dogs while you're there.

Bart Durham Injury Law: Better call Saul? More like better call Bart. The personal injury attorney was a true local celebrity (RIP) and the law firm he founded is still recognized counties over for its low-budget TV ads and highway billboards.

The Grumpy's Bail Bonds Woman: Another billboard superstar, Leah Hulan—better known as "the Grumpy's Bail Bonds Woman"—is the buxom blonde all Nashvillians call for their bail bond needs.

The Jugg Sisters: Real-life sisters Sheri Lynn and Brenda Kay play two oversexed cougars on Nashville's funniest and most outlandish musical comedy bus tour. Make sure to book in advance at NashTrash Tours as the Big Pink Bus sells out months in advance.

Manuel: Dubbed the "Rhinestone Rembrandt," fashion designer Manuel Cuevas—known simply as

"Manuel"—continues Nudie Cohn's legacy with his elaborate rhinestone and sequined suits. He is the man credited with putting Johnny Cash in black and helped make Elvis's famous gold lamé jumpsuit.

Santa: Our Santa is a chain-smoking war vet who is most famous for his Wedgewood-Houston establishment, Santa's Pub. Visit the double-wide trailer for some cheap beer and good karaoke.

Soccer Moses: Let my people goal! When not playing lead guitar for the Christian rock band Jars of Clay, Stephen Mason is leading the masses as Nashville SC's biggest superfan.

WSMV Snowbird: Longtime Nashvillians will remember the Muppet-like mascot as a fixture on Channel 4 announcing school closings during snowy winter mornings.

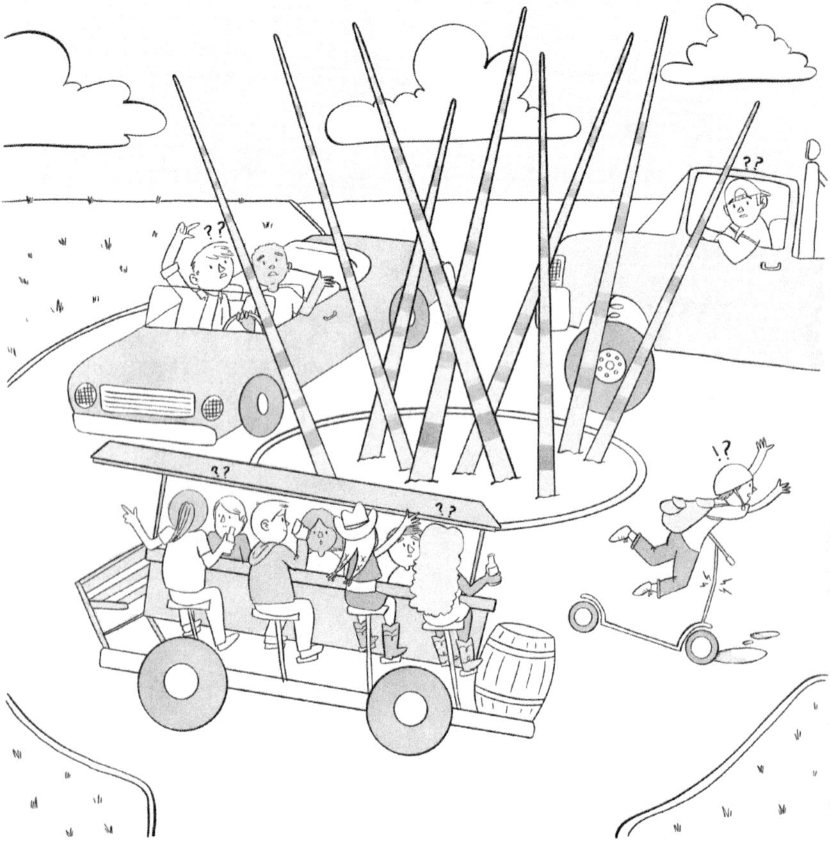

CHAPTER 3

Labyrinths, Potholes, and Cranes: A Nashville Driving Story

Whoever designed Nashville was drunk.

The city's streets are laid out in a labyrinth of concentric circles, each one more dizzying than the next. If, as a new driver, you constantly feel like you are navigating *around*, but never *toward*, your destination, then you know you have arrived. GPS won't help, it will only confound, and if you still believe the fastest way from Point A to Point B is straight, well, then you've never met anyone from TDOT.

To make matters worse, while driving along a street, you may notice that its name abruptly changes to something entirely different and then suddenly changes yet again to another name. Fear not. The same street makes a massive loop around town and its name can change multiple times. For instance, Old Hickory Boulevard turns into State Road 45, back into Old Hickory Boulevard, and then into Robinson Road, Old Hickory Boulevard again, back into State Road 45, and then finally, you guessed it, Old Hickory Boulevard. Fugitives on the run don't change identities this much. Here are some other examples:

- Walsh Road goes through the Fairgrounds and turns into Wedgewood Avenue, which turns into Blakemore Avenue, which becomes 31st Avenue South, which becomes 31st Avenue North, which becomes 28th Avenue North, which becomes Ed Temple Boulevard, which becomes Rosa L. Parks Boulevard, which becomes 8th Avenue South, which crosses Wedgewood (you just made a big loop) and becomes Franklin Pike.
- Harding Place turns into Battery Lane, which turns back into Harding Place, and then into Ezell Pike.
- Woodmont Boulevard turns into Thompson Lane, which turns into Briley Parkway, which turns into White Bridge Road, which turns back into Woodmont Boulevard.

Modes of Transportation

Car

Nashville is a driving city, and you are going to need a car, because . . .

Public Transport

We don't have any. Or rather, Nashville has a public transportation system the same way you or I have an appendix: it exists, but we never use it. Like sidewalks, it's the can we keep kicking down the road. Mayor Karl Dean proposed a seven-mile bus line called "the Amp." That was abandoned in 2015. Mayor Megan Barry proposed a twenty-six-mile light rail system called "Let's Move Nashville." That was rejected by Nashville voters in 2018. Current mayor Freddie O'Connell is a huge public transit advocate. We mourn for his "Choose How You Move" plan in advance.

Every administration comes up with a traffic study, and all it does is lead to more studies. We have studies about studies, each one revealing our traffic woes are worse than in the last study. Yet nothing ever seems to get done. So, here's hoping there's a monorail to the airport by 2060!

Bicycles
New bike lanes seem to pop up every day, and the nonprofit Walk Bike Nashville does a good job of making the city safer for bikers and walkers alike. However, Amsterdam we are not. You'll just as soon see someone on a Pedal Tavern as you will on a pedal bicycle. Which reminds us . . .

Road Hazards
Like any city, Nashville has its share of potholes and crazy drivers, but many of our road hazards tend to be a little more . . . unique to us.

Pedal Taverns
A pedal tavern—part bicycle, part pub—manages to annoy pedestrians and motorists alike. These slow-moving mobile pubs fueled by the collective pedaling power of their passengers provide the perfect blend of pseudo-exercise and public nuisance. Patrons struggle to maintain a steady pace while desperately trying to chug an overpriced beer. It's like a cross between a rambunctious pub crawl, a karaoke bar, and a very corrupt Tour de France.

If pedal taverns remained confined to a loop around downtown, most locals would be okay with them. But pedal taverns have started creeping beyond downtown into the 12 South and Vanderbilt areas, where they tie up traffic and create total chaos. All too often, riders get a little too drunk, tumble off, and suffer injuries. Somewhere, the executives of National Life and Accident would be proud.

Transportainment Vehicles

Another annoying road hazard is transportainment (a blend of "transportation" and "entertainment") vehicles. Examples include roofless old school buses, farm tractors, and wiener mobiles. Day and night, these licensed (and sometimes unlicensed) vehicles cruise the streets of downtown Nashville with flashing lights, revelers swaying and shimmying off the sides, and country music blasting from thumping speakers.

It's estimated more than forty companies operate the transportainment vehicles that clog up our narrow streets, turning our once-easy-going city known for outstanding live music into NashVegas. In 2021, the *New York Times* reported that the menagerie of party buses circling downtown Nashville included "a truck with a hot tub, a bus packed with electric massage chairs, a Ford pickup retrofitted into a 'party barge' with waves painted on the side and 'Ship Faced' stamped on the tailgate, retired military vehicles, a purple bus with drag performers, an old school bus adorned with horns named

Bev and yet another old bus with horns named Bertha." It's the world's most extravagant redneck motorcade.

Cranes

The construction boom in Nashville creates a perpetual maze of cranes and roadblocks. To help us navigate Nashville's explosive growth spurt, the *Nashville Business Journal* launched "Crane Watch" on its website (www.bizjournals.com/nashville/maps/nashville-crane-watch). Despite the interactive guide, sometimes driving around Nashville feels like a real-life game of Whack-A-Mole. Just when you think you've found a way around one construction site, you run smack into another, explaining why we consider the construction crane our official state bird.

Nine Naked People

It's not just the slow-moving party buses or construction zones you need to watch out for. Sometimes, our roadside artwork can be just as distracting. In 2003, Nashville installed *Musica*, a privately funded thirty-eight-foot-tall bronze sculpture of nine nude figures, male and female, dancing in a circle, in the Music Row Roundabout. It cost $1.1 million and was created by local artist Alan LeQuire, who previously sculpted the statue of Athena at the Parthenon in Centennial Park.

Despite the tasteful depiction of nudity, controversy ensued. Critics claim the naked figures are obscene, inappropriate for children, and unrelated to music. One local pastor argued privately funded depictions of nudity should not be displayed on public property if privately funded monuments of the Ten Commandments are legally prohibited. Pranksters occasionally dress the figures in everything from bell-bottom jeans to Predators jerseys. Country music songwriter Lee Thomas Miller even penned a tune in 2004 titled "Hillbilly Porn" with the chorus:

If it makes you think dirty, go ahead, honk your horn
Oh, the mayor done bought us some hillbilly porn.

That mayor, by the way, was not Bill Boner.

LeQuire's original design included a series of fountains surrounding the sculpture, but budget constraints, and perhaps a puritanical reluctance to bring more attention to the sculpture's state of undress, forced the city to scrap those plans. Finally, in 2016 a nonprofit group announced its intention to raise money to install fountains with choreographed water around the sculpture. At the time of writing this book, the fountains have yet to be installed.

Roundabouts

When we built our first roundabout in Music Row in the late 1990s, the Metro government access channel broadcast a four-minute video tutorial on how to drive around the rotary. Apparently, few residents saw the video and the Music Row Roundabout continues to provide a conundrum for drivers—as do all other roundabouts in Nashville today.

The Nashville way to use a roundabout is to wait until no cars are coming, enter into either of the two lanes, and exit from either lane—turning yourself into a Bart Durham dream client. The most notable of these is the *Stix* roundabout downtown, featuring a seventy-foot-tall sculpture made entirely of twenty-seven red cedar wood poles spaced in an irregular pattern and embedded at different angles. Most locals don't need the distraction created by a bunch of poles randomly jutting from the middle of a roundabout that they have enough difficulty navigating in the first place. Of course, maybe the city is just trying to give us a "crash course" in art appreciation.

Four-Way Stops

When we come to a four-way stop at the same time as another car, we wait and wait, then gesticulate at the same time as the other driver for them to go ahead, facilitating more waiting. If you've ever seen hometown comic Nate Bargatze's routine on this, then you know it ends with one of the drivers stepping outside their car and saying, "Guys, I'm out." The reality isn't too far off.

Crosswalks

If you're a pedestrian, beware: Nashville drivers pay no attention to crosswalks. Yes, you'll see the thick white stripes painted in the street, and pedestrians do have the legal right of way, but do not assume any oncoming cars or trucks will stop for you. The crosswalks merely provide the illusion of safety, like a lap belt on a school bus.

Honk If You're an Outsider (from California)

Locals almost never use their car horn. We give people a very long, very slow breath before ever honking. In fact, when we do hear a car horn, we can only assume the person is from out of town, probably California. Locals presume everybody who drives aggressively "must be from California." Why California? Why not one of the other forty-eight states? According to the US Census Bureau, only one in ten new residents in Tennessee moved here from California in 2022. Yet somehow, we still think only California transplants drive poorly.

Maybe we throw Californians under the (underutilized) bus because we stereotype Californians as New

Age nutjobs while we consider ourselves rooted in traditional values. Or maybe we're proud of our country music industry but we're secretly jealous of the entertainment industry in Hollywood and the tech industry in Silicon Valley. Or maybe we mistakenly blame Californians for our rising housing prices and all the gentrification in Nashville.

What is true is that people are moving here from all over and traffic is increasing as a result. It used to take fifteen minutes to get anywhere. Now it takes twenty-two. Still not bad by California standards.

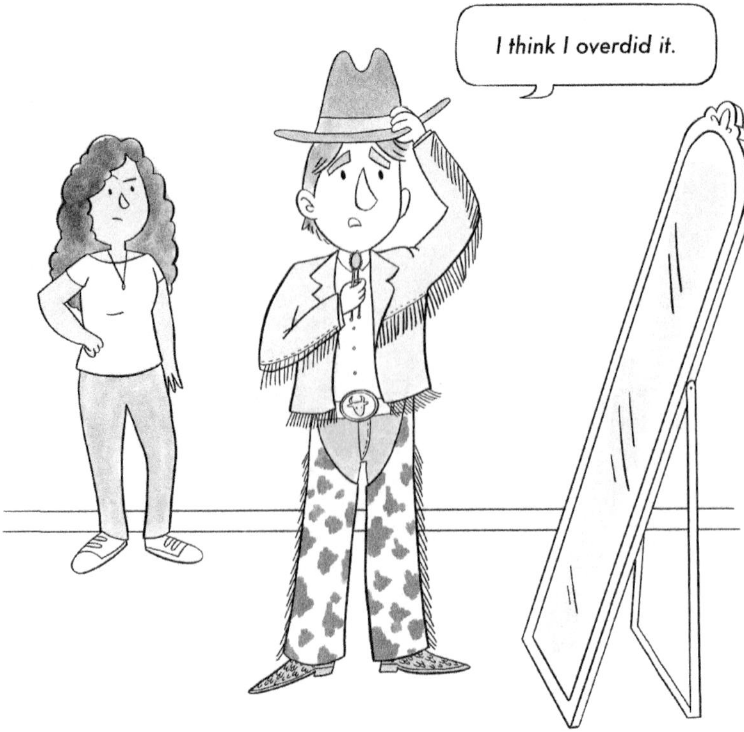
I think I overdid it.

CHAPTER 4

Rookie Mistakes to Avoid

If you see someone wearing a cowboy hat and boots in Nashville, that is a telltale sign they are from New Jersey.

It's an honest mistake. No one told these newcomers and tourists that few locals wear a cowboy hat or cowboy boots, accoutrements that are actually Texan or Western. If, for some reason, you must own a pair of cowboy boots, go to Boot Country at 304 Broadway, where you can buy one pair and get an additional two pairs for free. But we'd much prefer you read this chapter instead. It will guide you in avoiding some local faux pas during your first few months here.

Mispronouncing Things

We admit some of our city and street names are pronounced a little oddly. Here are a few that give newcomers fits, and how to actually pronounce them:

- Demonbreun [duh-MUN-bree-uhn]
- La Vergne [Luh-VERN]
- Lafayette [Luh-FAY-ett]
- Lebanon [LEB-uh-nun]
- Leiper's Fork [LEE-pers FORK]
- Murfreesboro [MUR-freeze-bur-row]
- Sevier [Suh-VEER]

Not Preparing for Allergy Season

If you begin taking a daily antihistamine in April, you're already too late.

Living in Nashville is like living on the surface of Planet Pollen. The city is located beneath the Cumberland Plateau, which means that when the winds pick up, the pollen doesn't clear out—it simply gets trapped. Add that to the fact that we get a lot of mold-producing rain, and the spring (and fall) can become a sneeze-fest for allergy sufferers. It's a wonder "God bless you" has yet to become our state motto.

To help alleviate the suffering, try starting that antihistamine routine in March. You can also purchase some local honey from one of our great farmers' markets in

12 South or Richland Park, or the main one downtown located next to Bicentennial Capitol Mall. It may or may not actually help, but it sure will be tasty.

Comparing Nashville and Memphis

Bless your heart. The age-old rivalry between Nashville and Memphis is like a dance-off between honky-tonk country and soulful blues. And while it may seem the two cities go toe-to-toe on certain things—Broadway vs. Beale Street, hot chicken vs. barbecue, country vs. blues—there is no comparison.

Please be kind to our redheaded stepchild to the west. They're doing the best they can.

Breaking the Musical Code

Depending on the show you're seeing at the Ryman, it may be frowned upon to stand up and dance. It's a former church, after all, and the pews sometimes give the performance a more formal concert vibe. Read the room before busting out your moves. Your neighbor behind you will thank you.

Then there's the "in-the-round." In Nashville, an in-the-round is a songwriting tradition that truly makes Nashville *Nashville*. At an in-the-round, a group of three or four songwriters share the stage, sit together in a circle, and take turns performing their original songs, typically on acoustic guitars. Each songwriter shares the story of how they wrote the song they're about to perform. It's a showcase for both up-and-coming artists and writers whose songs have topped the music charts. Some of the biggest names in music have participated in a Nashville in-the-round. It is a quintessential Nashville experience you should attend every time the opportunity presents itself.

But a big word of warning. Talking to your neighbor during a song is one of the biggest faux pas you can make at an in-the-round and you likely will receive a few incredulous stares from those around you. When the singer-songwriter performs, no one talks out of respect for the performer.

Celebrities, Name-Dropping, and Raising Hell
Here's another strict rule in Nashville: we do not bother the celebrities who live here. If you see them out, leave them alone. Name-dropping is kind of the kissing cousin to that behavior. It won't get you anywhere and will only serve to make people think, "New here?"

The same is true of yelling. If someone yells at us, we automatically shut down. So, if you do name-drop or unleash your inner diva at someone working for you, expect a cold shoulder or sudden project delays and supply-chain issues to rain down upon you. The next time you're feeling high and mighty, just remember that Nashville has a way of humbling oversized egos. Even the proudest peacocks learn to strut their stuff with a little more humility.

Snowplow Assumptions

Several years ago, a friend of mine moved here from the Northeast and a mild snowstorm fell over Nashville. "No big deal," he thought. "Come morning the street will be completely plowed."

By day three of being stuck inside, he had learned a valuable lesson. It's not the snow but the lack of snowplows that leads to Snowmageddon here. We're simply not equipped for it.

So, when the city loses its collective mind over a little dusting, just know it's an infrastructure issue and that cabin fever is incoming. That, or it'll melt the next day.

PART TWO: SETTING OUT

I'm seeing his arteries are filled with hot chicken.
VUMC
VUMC

CHAPTER 5

Eat, Drink, and Be Merry, for Tomorrow We're Hungover

When British Airways added nonstop service to Nashville from London in 2018, local reporters gathered at the airport for the inaugural flight, eager to interview disembarking passengers. "What brings you to our fair city?" they wanted to know.

"Dinner at the Catbird Seat," proclaimed one of the first people off the plane. "I heard it was an amazing restaurant, and I said I'd only come if there was a direct flight."

To longtime locals, the food scene's evolution is nothing short of a miracle. In the nineties, it was not uncommon for Pizza Hut and Red Lobster to be named in the *Nashville Scene*'s "Best of Nashville" poll. Now scores of James Beard–nominated chefs ply their trade in restaurants across the city, and people are flying across the Atlantic to eat here. It's a brave new world.

Restaurants run the gamut from the trendy to the old staples, from down-home cooking to international fare . . . and still many will argue nothing beats Waffle House or Cracker Barrel.

As for drink, we have plenty. New breweries and cocktail bars seem to pop up weekly, and if you think you need to haul it to Lynchburg, Tennessee or Kentucky for whiskey and bourbon, think again. There are a number of great distilleries right here in our own backyard.

Now that you've settled in, it's time to set out. Come along as we give you the lowdown on our culinary staples, starting with the one people (mainly tourists) can't seem to get enough of.

Hot Chicken

In the 1930s, Thornton Prince cheated on his girlfriend. Legend holds that she sought revenge by seasoning his fried chicken with excess spices. But rather than setting his taste buds on fire, her recipe inspired him to feature the dish in his restaurant. That's right, he *loved* it.

One bite of this chicken will transport you to the blazing abyss of Dante's Inferno . . . or it might just turn you on. According to Thornton's great-niece, Andre Prince, hot chicken often acts as an aphrodisiac. One customer in particular—a "lady of the evening"—was known for bringing her suitors to their old East Nashville location, where the duo would dine out before going home to do the deed. Well, one night they couldn't wait, and Prince and others looked up to see the lovebirds doing it on the hood of her car.

Whatever effect it has on you, now that you've moved here, you need to try it at least once. You can order hot chicken with varying degrees of intensity at:

- Prince's Hot Chicken, 5055 Broadway, Downtown
- Hattie B's, 2222 8th Avenue South, Melrose
- 400 Degrees, 3704 Clarksville Pike, Bordeaux
- Pepperfire, 5104 Centennial Boulevard, The Nations

Meat & Three

A Southern classic that is just what it sounds like: one meat and three sides. Usual suspects of the cafeteria-style eateries include country fried steak, chicken and dumplings, meatloaf, green beans, turnip greens, mac and cheese, mashed potatoes, and other foods that have kept our healthcare industry in business. You'll likely find all the vegetables smothered in butter and cream as we believe in turning even the healthiest greens into heart-stopping, artery-clogging works of art that would make a cardiologist cringe.

The late John Prine (RIP) was a regular at Arnold's Country Kitchen, while other meat & three staples include Monell's, Swett's, and Big Al's Deli, which claims to have "food so good you'll slap yo mamma!"

Barbecue
The smoke from our barbecue pits is an integral part of the Nashville skyline. We passionately debate the ideal smoking time, how different woods affect the taste, and which joint reigns supreme (some say Martin's, others say Edley's, and still others say Peg Leg Porker). After all, we take our brisket, ribs, and pulled pork seriously.

Goo Goo Clusters
In 1912, in a copper kettle at the Standard Candy Company at Clark Street and First Avenue in Nashville, company owner Howell Campbell Sr. and his plant supervisor Porter Moore invented the first candy bar to combine multiple ingredients—caramel, marshmallow nougat, fresh-roasted peanuts, and milk chocolate—into one delectable cluster. The name "Goo Goo," inspired by the baby-talk phrase, emphasized the gooey goodness of the candy.

Initially sold without wrappers under glass at drugstore candy counters, Goo Goo Clusters were eventually wrapped in tinfoil. The candy's first slogan ("Goo Goo! It's so good, people will ask for it from birth") helped sales take off, and this renowned delicacy became Nashville's most popular candy.

Grits

The mysterious Southern porridge made of ground corn and a generous dollop of butter warms the soul. Whether you like 'em plain, cheesy, sprinkled with bacon bits, or smothered in gravy like a guilty pleasure, grits are the unsung hero of breakfast, patiently waiting to soak up your regrets from the night before and give you the strength to face another day.

The NunBun

Speaking of breakfast, longtime locals fondly recall the time Nashville became an international media sensation with the "NunBun." In 1996, an employee of Bongo Java noticed his cinnamon bun slightly resembled the face of Mother Teresa. The image took on a life of its own in the pre-internet age, eventually causing Bongo Java to become "the most famous coffeehouse in the world." Mother Teresa herself wrote a letter to owner Bob Bernstein, kindly requesting they stop using her image. The "Immaculate Confection" was eventually stolen on Christmas Eve 2005, when a thief removed the hinges from the coffeehouse's front door and took nothing but the NunBun.

Sweet Tea

You know you're a Nashville local if you consider sweet tea one of the major food groups. There's nothing quite like sipping a glass of iced tea mixed with enough sugar to induce a diabetic coma. No wonder we always feel so energetic. Every corner restaurant, diner, and gas station proudly serves this Southern elixir.

The Wedge Salad

You can't walk into a classic Nashville restaurant without seeing the wedge on the menu, stealing the spotlight from all the other salads. We go crazy for this nutrient-deficient salad that comprises a quarter head of iceberg lettuce topped with bacon and diced tomatoes and dripping in creamy blue cheese dressing. Move over Caesar salad. The wedge is here to stay.

Caramel Cake

Whether savored at a family gathering, a local bakery, or a quaint diner, caramel cake fills us with joy. The velvety layers of moist cake, topped with caramel frosting, transport us to a place of pure bliss and remind us of the simple pleasures in life. The go-to spot for locals to buy this bakers' confection is Dessert Designs, but be forewarned: if you don't get your holiday order in several weeks before the big day, you'll sit listening to a prerecorded message telling you the ordering window has closed.

> **"Why the Line?"**
>
> Just taste the food at any one of these popular restaurants and you'll immediately understand why people line up outside the door:
>
> - **Biscuit Love:** A beloved breakfast spot, Biscuit Love is known for its heavenly biscuit creations and Southern-inspired dishes. The line here can be long, but it's well worth the chance to dig into "Bonuts" (biscuit donuts).
> - **Hattie B's Hot Chicken:** This famous hot chicken joint is loved by locals and tourists alike, resulting in lines that often snake out the door. The crispy, spicy goodness is worth the wait.
> - **The Loveless Cafe:** People line up for a taste of this joint's famous Southern comfort food: legendary biscuits, red-eye gravy, country ham, and delicious fried chicken.
> - **The Pancake Pantry:** A Nashville breakfast institution, The Pancake Pantry serves up a wide variety of delicious pancakes and other breakfast favorites. Be prepared for a line that stretches around the block on weekends.
> - **Prince's Hot Chicken:** A Nashville original, Prince's Hot Chicken is where the spicy hot chicken craze began. See p. 40 for the full story.

Local Beers

With a wide range of local breweries in Nashville, you'll find ales, lagers, stouts, IPAs, pilsners and more, each with its own unique flavor and style, that will have you saying "Bottoms up, y'all!" Speaking of bottoms, our first recommendation for a local brew is:

Ruby Red Ale (Fat Bottom Brewing): Brewed at their large indoor/outdoor space in the Nations, this delicious ale is a blend of perfectly balanced specialty malts.

Cumberland Punch (East Nashville Beer Works): Brace yourself for a knockout punch of fruity flavors.

Dos Perros (Yazoo Brewing Company): A beer so good, you'll be screaming "yahoo!" and begging for another round of this Mexican-style lager. Yazoo Brewing Company is named after the founder's hometown in Mississippi and is one of the original craft beer breweries in Nashville.

Homestyle (Bearded Iris Brewing): This hazy IPA is like a comfy couch for your taste buds, giving them a cozy and hoppy home to relax in. Don't worry, you won't see a bearded woman named Iris on the label. It's named after the Tennessee state flower.

The Rose (Black Abbey Brewing Company): Like a romantic ballad, this Belgian-style blonde ale will serenade your taste buds with floral and spicy notes that will make your heart skip a beat.

Southern Wit (Tennessee Brew Works): This tasty beer pairs perfectly with porch swings and polite conversations about the weather.

Thunder Ann (Jackalope Brewing Company): With a name like that, you'll feel like you're summoning thunderstorms with every sip of this apricot-infused pale ale.

Thanks again for hosting us. You sure you don't want to come to Broadway with us?
Not on your life.

CHAPTER 6

The Neon Lights of Broadway

It must be said that as locals, we rarely go down to Broadway. In fact, we avoid it like the plague.

It's not that we don't like Broadway. Many of us have had some memorable evenings downtown between First and Fifth Avenues. It's just . . . Do New Yorkers go to Times Square? Or New Orleanians to Bourbon Street? Or Las Vegans to the Strip? With the exception of the Ryman, Symphony Center, and Bridgestone Arena, Broadway has become the province of tourists. However, considering Broadway produces more tax revenue than any other road in the entire state, Broadway is extremely important to the local economy. So, for that reason alone, you should try to have a basic understanding of this honky-tonk tourist mecca. Here's what you need to know.

The Honky Tonk Highway

Nashville's Honky Tonk Highway is a stretch of vibrant bars located on lower Broadway that spill live music into the streets from ten a.m. to three a.m. Typically, there's no cover charge so you can save your money to throw a tip in the hat for the musicians. Live bands fill each honky-tonk with the sound of fiddles, steel guitars, and gritty vocals that tell tales of heartbreak, love, and the simple pleasures of a cold beer.

If you're lucky, you might catch a rising star or a surprise guest appearance from a well-known country artist. Willie Nelson, Kris Kristofferson, Gretchen Wilson, Dierks Bentley, and others began their careers on this very street. The atmosphere is lively, the dance floors are packed, and the bartenders are skilled in pouring the perfect whiskey shot to keep the party goin' and your tab a-runnin'. Statistically speaking, 50 percent of people who go down here have an awesome time. The other 50 percent wake up with a throbbing headache and a Bird scooter in their bed, wondering, "Why do I do this to my body?"

The most beloved and authentic venues include Robert's Western World (try the "Recession Special"), Tootsie's Orchid Lounge, the Stage on Broadway, Acme Feed & Seed, and Legends Corner.

CHAPTER 6

> **We're in the Wrong Business**
>
> Want to get an idea of how crazy real estate has gotten on Broadway? The building located at 411 Broadway—currently Garth Brooks's Friends in Low Places Bar & Honky-Tonk—was purchased in 2005 for $3 million. In 2021, Garth's people bought it for a whopping $47.9 million.
>
> Folks, we're in the wrong business.

Venturing Outside Broadway

It's only natural that after a few hours on Broadway, you may want to escape it.

A seven-minute walk up the road is Printers Alley, the most famous alley in Nashville. In the early 1900s, Printers Alley was home to two large newspapers, ten print shops, and thirteen publishers. When Prohibition went into effect in Tennessee in 1909, Printers Alley became home to a number of speakeasies and brothels, sparking a wild nightlife with risqué entertainment. Today, the bars and restaurants in Printers Alley generally open around six p.m. at the earliest. The highlights include Ms. Kelli's Karaoke Bar, Bourbon Street Blues and Boogie Bar, and a burlesque club called Skull's Rainbow Room.

Skull's Rainbow Room started in 1948 when David "Skull" Schulman opened his bar at the end of Printers

Alley. A flamboyant and flashy figure considered the "Mayor of Printers Alley," Schulman owned two poodles and wore Nudie jackets, *Hee Haw* overalls, rhinestones, and a belt buckle with a skull. Over the years entertainers including Elvis Presley, Johnny Cash, Etta James, Patsy Cline, Paul McCartney, and Bob Dylan have appeared on the Rainbow Room's legendary checkerboard stage.

In 1998, Schulman was killed at eighty years of age during a robbery in the club, resulting in the closure of the Rainbow Room for the next eighteen years. Today, Skull's Rainbow Room serves dinner and Sunday brunch, and features live jazz nightly and a burlesque show at eleven p.m. on Thursday, Friday, and Saturday nights.

> ### Karaoke Galore
> Ms. Kelli's in Printers Alley isn't the only place to channel your inner performer. Other go-to karaoke spots in the city include Santa's Pub, the Lipstick Lounge, and Sid Gold's Request Room.

Nashville's Most Famous Bathroom

The area surrounding Printers Alley is filled with boutique hotels like the Noelle, Bobby, and Dream, as well as the grand dame of Nashville hotels, the Hermitage.

CHAPTER 6

Stepping into the green-and-black Art Deco men's room in the lobby of the Hermitage Hotel, built in 1910, feels like entering a royal throne room fit for a country king. The opulent terrazzo flooring, intricate tile work, and two-seat shoeshine station showcase the hotel's commitment to timeless elegance. Nashville's ritziest restroom, voted America's Best Bathroom in 2008, is adorned with vintage sconces, polished brass fixtures, and plush leather seating, exuding a sense of indulgence and comfort. The attention to detail, from the meticulously maintained amenities to the fresh floral arrangements, reflects the hotel's dedication to providing an exceptional place to do your business.

In 2021, the historic hotel upped its game and unveiled a refurbished women's restroom, featuring some of the same design motifs as the men's room but with a cliché feminine touch: marble walls and floors striped in shades of pink, rose-gold-framed mirrors, and bright pink faucets.

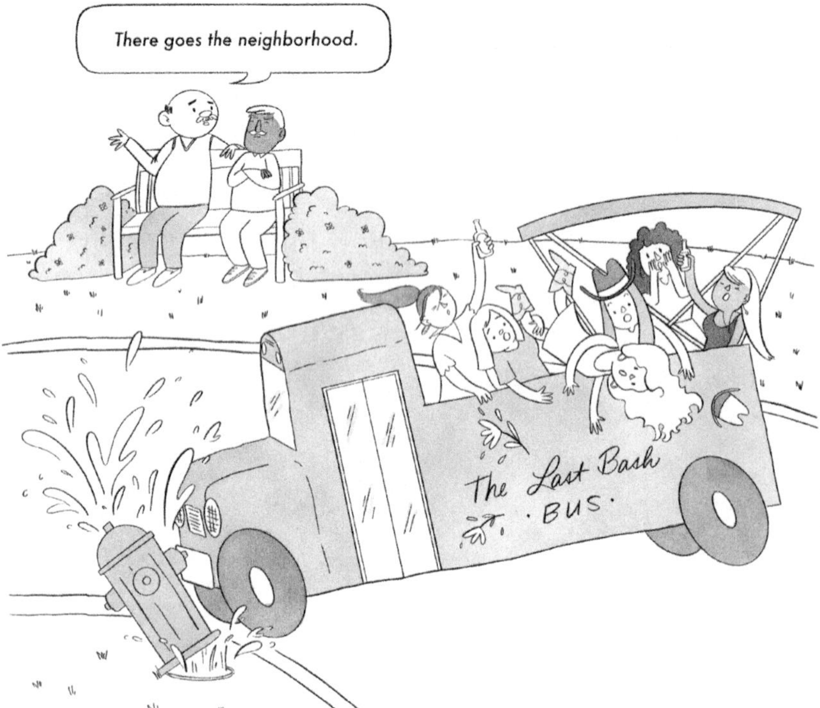
There goes the neighborhood.
The Last Bash
·BUS·

CHAPTER 7

Invasion of the Bachelorettes

In Nashville, they say you can't throw a rock without hitting a guy with a guitar. The same might be said for a girl with a sash.

Nashville has become the bachelorette capital of America, with thousands of women descending on the city every week. If you visit the Nashville airport on Thursday or Friday, the arriving gaggles of bachelorettes, clad in sparkling cowboy hats and matching pink sashes, look eager and excited about the fantastic weekend ahead. Come Sunday, you'll find those same bachelorettes now bleary-eyed and hungover, with sashes askew and mangled cowboy hats, sleeping on the airport floor to await their return flights home. Sure, it's a sad sight, but there's more to this story than meets the perfectly shadowed eye. So read on.

How to Spot a Bachelorette Party in Nashville (and What to Do If You Encounter One)

Since first arriving on the scene around the mid-2010s, bachelorettes have become among our most conspicuous of weekend imports. Their uniform typically consists of pink sequined cowboy hats, white cowboy boots, pink feathered boas, Daisy Dukes, and fringed glitter T-shirts. Often these shirts will come printed with cutesy slogans like "Let's Get Nashty," "Last Bash in Nash," or "Smashed in Nash." You will see them rolling by on open-air party buses, leaning over the railings and swaying to amplified music as they down another Jell-O shot. From miles away, locals can identify them by their signature rallying cry, a high-pitched and triumphant "WOOOOOOOO!!!"

So, what to do if you encounter a "woo girl" in the wild? After all, the groups we get tend to be a bit rowdy. They often come wielding a wide variety of penis-shaped novelties, such as penis hats, penis straws, penis squirt guns, penis pacifiers, penis drinking cups, penis piñatas, and the pièce de résistance, a large inflatable penis float for their Airbnb pool. Needless to say, brides-to-be looking for a relaxing spa weekend do not choose Nashville.

Luckily, your chances of physically encountering them are fairly slim. Most bachelorette groups stick together, and as long as they stay downtown, we locals don't make a big fuss. Even their short-term rentals tend to be concentrated in one area (there's a "bachelorette village" around Edgehill). But once they're here, we can't control where else they might venture. Recently, I was enjoying brunch in Green Hills when a gaggle of bachelorettes walked in, and no one could believe they had strayed that far from downtown. It's like seeing a report on the local news about a bear or mountain lion that's wandered into a subdivision and thinking, "Huh, how'd that make its way here?"

So What's the Verdict?
Many locals bemoan that bachelorettes represent all that is wrong with twenty-first-century Nashville. "Old Nashville" versus "New Nashville" is how it is usually framed. It's the preservation (or lack thereof) of what made Nashville cool, like the Ryman Auditorium and Robert's Western World, colliding up against experience-driven traps like the angel's-wings mural or any number of the new celebrity-backed bars. We can't seem to accept—or don't seem to like—that the city would bend to their will in such a branded, inauthentic way.

These locals are absolutely right about the bachelorettes, but they're also great for the local economy. The bachelorettes spend gobs of money. They've created an entire industry and a reliable revenue stream for locals whose livelihoods now depend on them, pumping millions of dollars each year into the city. Those tourist dollars pay to prevent our potholes from swallowing small cars whole and replace all the stolen "Welcome to Nashville" signs that now decorate college dorm rooms.

What's more, an estimated one thousand bachelorettes descend on Nashville each weekend—which is a lot, but it means they make up less than 1 percent of overall tourists. So, the hype is probably bigger than the reality.

The bottom line is, bachelorettes are coming whether we like it or not. We remember that there's nothing wrong with women enjoying each other's company for a celebratory weekend. We try to extend our friendliness to make them feel right at home—penis-shaped party favors and all.

I don't even mind.

CHAPTER 8

The Music Scene

Once you start giving directions using music venues as landmarks, you know you've become a local.

> *"Elliston Place Soda Shop? Just go past the Exit/In and it'll be on your right."*

> *"Head down Hillsboro Pike. If you pass the Bluebird, you've gone too far."*

> *"I just drove by the Basement, so I'm about five minutes away."*
> *"The Basement or Basement East?"*
> *"Beast."*

Live music is in our lexicon, and we're fortunate to have access to a plethora of venues putting out some of the best live music in the country. Seven nights a week, you can catch a concert, hear a band in a bar, or drop in on an open mic night at one of the 180 music venues in town. But it all starts and ends with one place.

The Ryman Auditorium

Home of the *Grand Ole Opry* from 1943 to 1974, the Ryman Auditorium is the holy grail of music venues. In 1956, Johnny Cash met June Carter backstage and told her he knew they'd marry one day. Twelve years later, they did. We locals similarly get swept up in emotion whenever we're in the Mother Church.

Founded in 1892 as the Union Gospel Tabernacle, the Ryman hosts a diverse range of performances, captivating audiences with its timeless charm and unmatched acoustics. You'll be moved by the stained-glass windows and wooden pews inside this living testament to the power of music.

At one point the Ryman fell into disrepair and came close to being demolished, but fortunately a team of musicians and Nashville residents rallied together to save and restore the historic site as an active music venue downtown.

Trust us, visits here are well worth breaking the local rule never to go downtown. It's just that good.

But beware, not all seats are created equal in this iconic spot. If you don't choose your seats wisely, you might be stuck watching a column all night instead of your favorite band.

The Opry House

The *Grand Ole Opry* moved from the Ryman to its own permanent home in 1974. Called the Opry House, it's a giant sanitized version of the Ryman specifically designed for the legendary show and located roughly ten miles outside of town. Despite the soulless aesthetics, it continues to bring the best of country music to the world, preserving its rich traditions while embracing new generations of talented artists. Will you ever go there? Maybe once or twice, but it's more likely you'll make the trek out there to see the holiday lights at the Opryland Resort and Convention Center.

Within walking distance of the Opry House sits the Opryland Resort and Convention Center, a monstrous facility that makes the Mall of America look quaint. With 2,888 hotel rooms, a river that runs through it, more than fifteen restaurants and lounges, retail shops, and a four-acre water park, it is a touristy mash-up somewhere between the Venetian and EPCOT.

Music Row

It's one thing to enjoy music in Nashville. It's quite another to work in it.

Country singer-songwriter Ashley McBryde once joked that making music in Nashville "could feel like adopting a street cat, only to have it bite you when it turned out to be a possum." That possum is the country music machine, and it's headquartered on Music Row, which consists of the two parallel streets of Music Square East and Music Square West, and is where aspiring songwriters hold on tight to the hope of writing a hit.

In this part of town, deals are made, dreams are realized, and hopes are shattered. Record producers, songwriters, music publishers, and musicians regularly traffic here, while the industry as a whole supports $3.2 billion of labor income annually. Nashville has a higher concentration of people working in the music industry per capita than anywhere else in the world, and it shows.

Your hairdresser? You better believe they've written a heart-wrenching song about lost love.

Your server? You guessed it: part-time session drummer.

And your plumber? That man is country music. He lives and breathes whiskey and wild women.

Music Row is also a place of historical significance. RCA Studio B is where the "Nashville Sound" originated, and artists like Chet Atkins, Dolly Parton, and

Roy Orbison have all recorded there. The King himself, Elvis Presley, recorded more than two hundred songs at Studio B, including "Are You Lonesome Tonight," "It's Now or Never," and "How Great Thou Art." In June 1970, following his triumphant comeback in Las Vegas, Elvis returned to Studio B to record more than thirty songs in a five-day marathon session.

However, like many historically significant places, Music Row is under threat of the wrecking ball. It's been named one of America's Eleven Most Endangered Historic Places, with more than fifty demolitions taking place between 2013 and 2019. To put that into perspective, between 2000 and 2012 the number was only thirteen.

Music City vs. City of Music

One point of note: you've perhaps noticed Nashville's nickname "Music City." This is not to be confused with "the City of Music," which belongs to Vienna.

Vienna has Mozart and Beethoven and the Wiener Musikverein. We have Little Jimmy Dickens, Minnie Pearl, and Kid Rock's Big Ass Honky Tonk Rock 'n' Roll Steakhouse.

Some people say Europe is more refined than America, but we'll hear none of it.

Unique Listening Opportunities

Nashville is more than just country covers played downtown. Here are some unique musical opportunities to check out in neighborhoods near you:

In-the-Round: You've probably never heard the names or seen the faces of any of the performers before (unless you're in the music business), but I promise you probably already know some of their songs by heart. Oftentimes, you wouldn't think these musicians had ten cents to their name. They wear T-shirts, shorts, and flip-flops, and look like they just rolled out of bed, but they've usually had at least one song hit the charts. As a local, one of the best places to experience an in-the-round is at the Bluebird Cafe. Unfortunately, the television show *Nashville* featured the Bluebird and now tourists flock to the tiny venue, making it difficult to get one of the ninety seats. However, multiple times a year the Bluebird also hosts Bluebird on the Mountain at the Vanderbilt Dyer Observatory, which seats several hundred people, but please keep this spectacular alternative secret from the tourists.

Movie Night at the Schermerhorn: For a truly incredible acoustic experience, check out the Schermerhorn Symphony Center's movie concert series. Select evenings throughout the year, our Grammy Award–winning symphony plays the full soundtrack to such masterpieces as *Star Wars*, *E.T.*, and *Jurassic Park*—all while the film screens on a projector behind them. The highlight is *Home Alone* in Concert during the holidays.

Honky Tonk Tuesdays: Every Tuesday at the American Legion Post 82 Inglewood, travel back in time for a little country-western swing deep in the heart of East Nashville. If it's too packed, head up the road to Dee's Country Cocktail Lounge. And if it's not Tuesday, head back down the road for something entirely different at Motown Monday at The 5 Spot.

Full Moon Pickin' Party: Held monthly from May to September at Percy Warner Park, the city bills this as "one of Nashville's most popular outdoor events, attracting families, friends, and dog lovers from all over to hear local musicians play together under the full moon, in one of Nashville's most picturesque settings."

Swan Ball? Is that like an endangered animal benefit?
Not exactly.

CHAPTER 9

The Nashville Social Calendar

To add to your busy social calendar, here is a list of some notable events all new locals should know about:

MARCH
30A: For spring break, hordes of pale Nashvillians make the annual mass migration south to 30A, a scenic highway located in the Florida Panhandle that stretches along the coastline of the Gulf of Mexico and passes through several picturesque beach communities. Nashville empties out as everyone you know goes to get away from everyone they know, and then all of them hang out together on 30A. Those Nashville locals who remain in town get the opportunity to enjoy the serenity of traffic-free streets and shorter lines at local brunch spots. While

Instagram feeds fill up with sun-kissed selfies, Nashville locals embrace the peace and quiet of not having to fight for a parking spot. Word to the wise: if you end up in Panama City, Panama, you took the wrong flight.

APRIL
Rock 'n' Roll Nashville Marathon and Half Marathon: For the cardio inclined, every year the city transforms into a massive running party as thousands of participants hit the streets for a marathon, half marathon, 10K, and 5K run. Our city comes alive with passionate runners from all over the world, conquering the course while taking in the great sights of Nashville. After the race, the good times continue with a country music concert, because in Music City, the best way to celebrate completing a marathon is with live music and a little dancing. If your legs haven't fallen off yet, they should after this.

MAY
Steeplechase: The annual Iroquois Steeplechase, our big fundraiser for the Children's Hospital at Vanderbilt, is a full day of horse races held on the second Saturday in May. Some twenty-five thousand spectators descend on Percy Warner Park decked out in extravagant hats and seersucker suits to watch horses race, but mostly to drink. Even the horses seem a little drunk as they hurdle hedges

at an alarmingly unsuccessful rate. It's basically just a big society party with old-fashioned wicker picnic baskets, good china, and silverware, like an Ole Miss tailgate party. There's fancy box seating, open bars, shaded tents, and the green grass hill where attendees can sit on a blanket and enjoy the day. Between the horse races, little kids (not drunk) compete in a footrace on hobby horses and attendees watch the popular Parade of Hounds.

To enhance the enjoyment of the event, people often bet by putting the horses' names on small pieces of paper (or cutting them from the program) and placing them into a decorative hat or container. After everyone bets (often $5), each person then randomly selects a horse name from the hat to cheer on during the next race, ensuring a fair distribution but making the winner of each race completely luck of the draw.

It invariably rains during the Steeplechase, so be prepared to wear wellies with that beautiful dress and big hat.

Tennessee Renaissance Festival: Ever wanted to witness grown adults earnestly engaging in mock sword fights while consuming turkey legs the size of their own heads? At this anachronistic event held every weekend in May, Nashville locals can escape the monotony of modern life by pretending they're in a world where Wi-Fi doesn't exist and corsets are a viable fashion choice.

JUNE

CMA Music Festival: Formerly known as Fan Fair, CMA Fest has a rich history that dates back to 1972, when it was first held at Nashville's Municipal Auditorium and attracted five thousand fans. What started as a way for country music fans to meet their favorite artists has since grown into a four-day extravaganza. The festival can draw upwards of ninety thousand fans daily, who come from all fifty states and nearly fifty countries to hear more than one hundred fifty featured artists. From ten a.m. to midnight every day, bands perform on temporary stages set up all over town, and major acts play the stadiums. Most artists try to be extremely accessible and accommodating since fans stand in line for hours just to get an autograph or selfie. Fortunately, the fans confine themselves to downtown, so they can walk to the different venues, but the whole city still feels transformed into a nonstop party, with live music echoing from every corner.

For locals, CMA Fest should really be declared a four-day holiday as we all try to flee town before the throngs of country music fans descend on us. If we're unlucky enough to find ourselves in town, then we try to embrace the chaos and the influx of tourists, knowing that for a few days, Nashville becomes the epicenter of the music universe. It reminds us why we fell in love with Nashville in the first place—its passion for music and the way it brings people together in harmony, even if the snarled traffic turns downtown into a demolition derby for a few days.

Bonnaroo: In 1969, music-loving hippies descended on a muddy field in upstate New York for what would become the renowned Woodstock festival. Then in 2002, the organizers of the Bonnaroo Music and Arts Festival replicated that magical experience in Manchester, Tennessee—sixty-five miles southeast of Nashville. Year after year, Bonnaroo lures in more and more people with promises of music, peace, and questionable hygiene practices. The four-day event, steeped in tradition, unites people in their love for bands, sweltering heat, overpriced food trucks, and endless porta-potty lines.

JULY

Fourth of July: Our downtown fireworks show has become one of the biggest in the nation. Thousands gather along the Cumberland River to witness the massive pyrotechnics display. Many locals opt to avoid this Fourth of July pilgrimage, which has become a tourist attraction, and instead decide to enjoy one of the smaller firework shows put on by local country clubs.

Hot Chicken Festival: Every Fourth of July, Nashville locals and tourists eagerly line up for hours to celebrate the joys of setting their taste buds on fire and pretend it's a profound culinary experience.

Jefferson Street Jazz and Blues Festival: On the third Saturday in July, locals gather at Tennessee State University's Edward S. Temple Track to hear the soulful sounds of jazz and blues fill the air, capturing the essence of Nashville's vibrant music scene.

AUGUST

Tomato Art Fest: One weekend every August, locals gather to celebrate the pinnacle of artistic expression through the medium of tomatoes. Adults paint, sculpt, and parade with squishy, overripe tomatoes, reminding us that this fruit masquerading as a vegetable deserves its fifteen minutes of fame.

SEPTEMBER

Live on the Green: Public Square Park transforms into a free concert series where we all enjoy many bands only listeners of Lightning 100 have ever heard of.

Americanafest: This annual event brings together thousands of Americana music fans and artists from all over the world. It feels like every bar in town is helping host these incredible acts, which play for five straight nights.

Nashville Film Festival: This weeklong film festival is one of the longest-running film festivals in the country, taking place every mid-to-late September at multiple venues around the city. Californians longing for a taste of home can catch a Hollywood-style production or a Tennessee-made short, with plenty of music films in between.

OCTOBER

Oktoberfest: The joyful sounds of music, the clinking of beer steins, and the scent of scrumptious bratwurst fill the streets. Friends and families gather in the heart of Germantown to relish a festive fusion of Southern charm and Bavarian flair.

Trick-or-Treating in Richland: In the historic Richland–West End neighborhood, considered ground zero for Halloween (thanks, sidewalks!), homeowners go all out in decorating their homes and handing out tons of candy to kids in costume. Neighbors put hundreds of carved pumpkins on display and turn their front yards into spooky graveyards that keep away the bad spirits of housing developers.

NOVEMBER

Boulevard Bolt: On Thanksgiving morning, people dress up as turkeys, Santas, pilgrims, reindeer, and just regular people to run/walk five miles down Belle Meade Boulevard to raise funds to benefit our homeless community. It's a great way to burn calories before spending the rest of the day eating and watching football.

DECEMBER

Mailbox Decorations: Starting December 1, tons of locals decorate their mailboxes with greenery and ribbons displaying varying levels of holiday spirit, making the neighborhoods feel remarkably jolly. As a newcomer, if you want to fit in like a local, you should definitely decorate your mailbox. If you're not up to the challenge, you can actually hire a local company to decorate your mailbox for you. If you can't afford a local company to decorate your mailbox for you, now is the time to take out a loan.

Holiday Lights at Opryland: Opryland sets up a massive holiday light display with more than four million lights, towering Christmas trees, fountain and light shows, over-the-top décor, and ice sculptures hand-carved from more than two million pounds of ice. The resort also features nightly tree lightings, carriage rides, ice tubing, seasonal dining and drinks, and all sorts of outdoor activities. Families from the surrounding counties hop in their cars and line up bumper-to-bumper for miles along Briley Parkway to inch toward the Opryland holiday display. Be aware, however, most locals wouldn't be caught dead there. If a houseguest wants to go see the Christmas lights at Opryland, just hand them your car keys and wish them the best of luck.

New Year's Eve: Locals are somewhat stunned that we're suddenly one of a handful of US cities seen on national television on New Year's Eve. We can't believe our New Year's celebration has grown that large. In 2023, a record 210,000 people attended the Big Bash at Bicentennial Capitol Mall. The free event, sponsored by Jack Daniel's, features a lineup of country music performers, the drop of a sixteen-foot-tall red neon musical note at midnight (similar to the ball drop in New York's Times Square), and a short but spirited fireworks display.

***

Charity Ball Madness

New to Nashville? Want to make fast friends in high places and support a good cause at the same time? Get out your checkbook. Charity galas are the lifeblood of the Nashville social scene. If you've got the dough, have we got the parties for you!

Of course, the dress code at these formal events typically requires white tie, black tie, cocktail attire, or general Bond villain. For women, there is the obligatory spray tan. If you're not up for going out, you can hire someone to spray you in the privacy of your home. If you can't afford someone to come to your house, again, consider a loan. Only Once in a Blue Moon, an annual gala that benefits the Land Trust (to conserve Tennessee's landscapes), encourages boots and jeans. Most of these formal events host auctions where you can bid on unique items like one-on-one songwriting lessons with a renowned songwriter, signed guitars by music heavyweights, original handwritten lyrics of country songs, or private concerts for a small group of family and friends.

Keep in mind not all charity balls are created equal. The cutthroat world of giving away your money begins with entry-level parties. These include the Heart Gala (a fundraiser for the American Heart Association), the Tennessee Waltz (for the Tennessee State Museum), and the TPAC Gala (for the Tennessee Performing Arts Center). These black-tie soirees will take anyone's money and give you the exposure you need to work your way up to the more exclusive invite lists for La Bella Notte (the annual gala to support the Nashville Opera), the Hermitage Gala (to preserve the historic home of President Andrew Jackson), and the Cause for Paws luncheon (a benefit for the Nashville Humane Association). Slip into a designer dress or finely tailored tuxedo, work the room, rub elbows with old money, become a patron-level donor, and—*voilà!*—you just might find your name on the invite list for the more exclusive Frist Gala (to benefit the Frist Art Museum), and Ballet Ball (to subsidize the Nashville Ballet), and possibly even the Symphony Ball (a white-tie event to bankroll the Nashville Symphony). Buy a case of cabernet sauvignon at the Nashville Wine Auction's annual l'Eté du Vin Gala to support the fight against cancer and your heightened social standing is all but guaranteed.

In Nashville, you can pay to play pretty much every weekend, but the belle of philanthropy balls is definitely the posh Swan Ball, a glamorous white-tie gala held in June at the Cheekwood Estate and Gardens with a three-course meal, wine, headliner entertainment, and an auction. The Swan Ball makes all the other charity balls pale in comparison. To break the barrier into this over-the-top, expensive, crème de la crème social event, potential invitees must be recommended by no less than three current names on the invite list.

PART THREE: GOING NATIVE

NASHVILLE WEATHER FORECAST
FRI
SAT
SUN
You can expect to enjoy typical spring weather conditions this weekend.

CHAPTER 10

Mother Nature— an Uneasy Relationship

According to the Nashville Visitor Center, "Nashville typically enjoys a mild and pleasant climate with only a few days of the year having either very hot or very cold conditions." Which is about as true as saying, "The South Pole can get chilly, bring a jacket."

So let us state it plain: Nashville is oppressively hot, the allergies are the worst, and the chiggers, they bite. So if the booze, bachelorettes, and brisket don't kill you, the weather here very well may. Here's a guide to surviving it all like a true native.

The Seasons

Summer: If you come from a place where you have to install those pesky window AC units every summer, the good news is central air-conditioning is the norm here. The bad news is central air-conditioning is the norm here.

Summer in Nashville is a certified hate crime. The temperature and the humidity are often the same number, and as our lawns wither away and our electricity bills skyrocket, we desperately crank up the air-conditioning to prevent our bedrooms from feeling like convection ovens.

To complicate matters, when it's 100 degrees Fahrenheit outside, it's 50 degrees Fahrenheit inside every restaurant, store, and movie theater. So pack a sweater and know that the moment you step outside, you're going to begin defrosting like a frozen rack of ribs. If you survive your first summer here and decide to stay, you're officially one of us.

Fall: We have fall in Nashville. Or rather, we have an identity crisis masquerading as fall. The fluctuating temperature feels like autumn, summer, and winter—often within the same week. All the attendant joys of the season still exist—foliage, SEC football, pumpkin carving—it just comes with a little sweating is all. Sweaty sweater weather, you might say.

To experience fall on steroids, locals often head to Cheekwood for the Cheekwood Harvest, highlighted by a photo in front of the Pumpkin Village. It is also the perfect time for a windows-down drive to Leiper's Fork, where one can cozy up to the fire and listen to live music at Fox & Locke.

Winter: Behold! The color gray! During winter, overcast skies blanket Nashville. Not that it matters: the sun seems to set at noon and the temperature consistently hovers between 35 and 40. We're located in the Central time zone, but we're a stone's throw from the Eastern time zone, so we get robbed of an extra hour of daylight. It's like we get all the bad parts of winter with none of the good parts. Or, in other words, it gets just cold enough to almost never snow.

Nashville receives an average of a mere 4.7 inches of snowfall a year. When snow does threaten to fall, the schools instantly shut down for no real reason and residents rush to the grocery stores to buy up all the bread and milk. Why bread and milk? Because we want to survive, just not for that long.

Yep, we freak out at the mere possibility of snow. The slightest bit of actual snow turns Nashville into a disaster zone (see chapter 4). We don't know how to drive in the snow, and yet many of us insist on venturing out, skidding into otherwise avoidable car accidents. If you want to play it safe, stay home, wait for the snow and ice to melt, and enjoy the spectacle from the comfort of your fuzzy slippers.

Spring: We get more inches of annual rainfall than Seattle, although Seattle gets more rainy days than we do (152 per year compared to our 119). The fickle temperatures make the great outdoors feel like winter, spring, and summer—often on the same day. Despite the fact that we're warned by every nursery in town not to buy any plants until April 15, the beautiful weather in March lulls us into buying them and then a hard freeze in early April kills them all. Beware: in spring, the aroma of blooming flowers and the sweet melodies of chirping birds perfectly mask the relentless assault of pollen on our sinuses. True locals know that to survive, one must begin taking daily allergy pills by early March or it's already too late (see chapter 4 again).

Surviving the Elements
We don't know what Nashville's ancestors did to upset the weather gods but Mother Nature seems to have it out for us. What we lack in hurricanes, earthquakes, and wildfires we make up for in flooding, tornadoes, and a murderer's row of insects. Heck, the Ten Plagues look quaint by comparison.

The Buzz on Insects
In Africa, the Big Five are the lion, leopard, rhinoceros, elephant, and buffalo.

CHAPTER 10

In Nashville, the Big Three are the mosquito, tick, and chigger.

Come summer, mosquitoes supply Nashville's unofficial soundtrack at dusk. These tiny airborne vampires ruin picnics, barbecues, and any outdoor gathering that features exposed skin. They have a knack for making even the most stoic individual break out in a frantic dance routine, turning a serene evening into a chaotic symphony of slaps and expletives. During mosquito season, arm yourself with bug spray, citronella candles, and a sense of humor. If your home has a porch and you wish to enjoy it, screen some of it to prevent the area from turning into an all-you-can-eat buffet.

Ticks—tiny, bloodsucking arachnids—are another uninvited guest that love to crash outdoor parties and picnics. With their knack for finding the perfect hiding spots in grassy areas and wooded trails, they wait for their chance to latch on to unsuspecting victims. Since these stealth critters transmit unwanted souvenirs like Lyme disease, they prompt locals to perform awkward tick-checking rituals that would astonish a contortionist. So, if you find yourself venturing into Nashville's great outdoors, make sure to armor up with tick repellent and protective clothing.

Chigger bites, another delightful souvenir gifted to us by the Nashville outdoors, cause intense itchiness and unsightly red spots. Like ticks, you can get chiggers by simply walking through any wooded or grassy area. Fortunately, scratching the skin causes these pesky mites to fall off, but the itch they leave remains for days. To soothe the itching, dab on calamine lotion or take an antihistamine like Benadryl.

Remember, the path to peace and tranquility in the Nashville outdoors might have a few bumps and itches along the way, but it's all part of the joy of nature.

Cicada Invasions
Every thirteen and seventeen years, billions of cicadas emerge from the earth and transform our city into a cacophony of buzzing and loud, shrill droning. Every attempt to enjoy nature becomes a nightmarish game of dodging flying cicadas as they swoop like kamikazes into our unsuspecting faces. These creepy insects cover every tree branch and streetlamp, and we can't walk anywhere without feeling the crunch of their discarded exoskeletons underfoot, like walking on Bubble Wrap to a horror movie soundtrack. When the cicadas finally retreat, we're left with the traumatic memory of Swarmageddon, dreading their inevitable return.

Torturous Trees
In the fall, the leaves of hackberry trees secrete a sticky

black saplike substance that coats our cars, requiring a scrub brush to wash it off, along with the paint finish. The black goo reminds us that mosquitoes and oppressive heat are sometimes the least of our problems, and that we're only as good as our last car wash.

When not dealing with sticky fingers and stubborn ooze on our cars and patios, we must also contend with Osage orange trees. Those unfortunate enough to park their cars beneath these seemingly beautiful trees might wake up with a cracked windshield or dent on their hood, as the five-pound, softball-sized "oranges" (which are actually green) love to fall in all the wrong places.

Tornadoes and Floods

An average of seventeen tornadoes touch down in Middle Tennessee each year. On March 3, 2020, three deadly tornadoes hit the area, damaging and destroying homes and businesses, killing more than twenty people.

Nashville's Outdoor Tornado Warning System operates tornado sirens at 113 public gathering places throughout the city. The sirens sound like Cold War air-raid warnings and signify that Doppler radar has identified a tornado or a trained spotter has seen a funnel cloud or tornado in progress. All sirens are tested at noon on the first Saturday of each month, but few people know the test schedule, making it difficult to determine whether the city is testing the sirens or if a tornado is headed straight for you.

Locals typically stand around asking each other, "Is that a tornado siren? Should we do something?" We basically treat tornado sirens like a fire alarm going off in a college dormitory. We figure it's probably nothing, but historically, a tornado may be about to strike. If you're anywhere near a golf course and sirens go off, the sirens could be warning about a tornado or lightning. It really makes no difference because everyone just continues with whatever they were doing. We tend to ignore the alarms. We don't know why. We're idiots on this topic, so please don't follow our lead here.

What are less easy to ignore are the torrential downpours that sometimes lead to flooding. In 2010, Nashville experienced its thousand-year flood when over thirteen inches of rain fell on the city between May 1 and 2. Twenty-six people lost their lives, and more than $2 billion in private property damage and $120 million in public infrastructure damage was recorded. At the Schermerhorn Symphony, which was covered in twenty-four feet of water, two Steinway grand pianos valued at more than $100,000 each were destroyed.

If there's a silver lining to any of these events, it's that Nashvillians come together during times of tragedy. When the 2010 floodwaters engulfed parts of the city, the mantra "Nashville Strong" stuck. The city and its people always bounce back.

> **@NashSevereWx**
>
> When bad weather looms, Nashvillians instinctively turn to Nashville Severe Weather (@NashSevereWx). The community-supported local weather account is run by dedicated "tweeteorologists" Will, David, Andrew, and Luke, who keep their three hundred thousand (and counting) followers safe and informed during severe weather events.

Please don't throw me!
NASHVILLE PREDATORS
PREDS
NASHVILLE PREDATORS

CHAPTER 11

The Pain of Being a Nashville Sports Fan

To be a sports fan in Nashville is to know pain.

We are blessed with three professional franchises, spoiled with some of the best facilities, and have a state-of-the-art Super Bowl–caliber stadium coming. And yet, zero championships. (Sure, the Vanderbilt baseball and bowling teams might take issue with that, to say nothing of Ed Temple's TSU Tigerbelles track-and-field team, but stick with me.)

The road to victory hasn't always been an easy one, but fans here are loud and proud and they punch above their weight. So hop on the fan bandwagon, there's plenty of room!

Tennessee Titans (NFL)
Just like Nashville weather, the Titans are unpredictable and prone to thunderous disappointment. Remember Tom Hanks' line in *Cast Away*? The one where he says, "Just let me get one thing straight: we have a pro football team now, but they're in *Nashville*?" Yeah, he said that derisively.

But it's better than it used to be. For a long time, the Titans were the punching bag of the NFL, and when people wonder what put New Nashville on the map, it wasn't just the ABC soap opera or the *New York Times* labeling us an "it city." It was also Chicago Bears fans filling up Nissan Stadium in 2012, cheering their team to a 52–20 victory, and then walking across the river to Broadway and almost drinking Nashville dry.

That's right. They completely drained many of our beloved bars of their beer supply.

From that point forward, our fate was sealed. Nashville became known as a hoppin' town (pun intended) and other teams' fan bases wanted in on the action, much to the chagrin of Titans fans and their players.

T-Rac, the team's mascot, is a raccoon that rides a four-wheeler on the field during time-outs. God help us all.

Nashville Predators (NHL)
One might not think of Nashville as a hockey town, but one would be wrong. We Prednecks love our hockey

team, even if the majority of us still don't know what "icing" is. When the organization first arrived in 1997, team officials set up a kiosk at the CoolSprings Galleria to show locals hockey highlights and teach us the rules of the game. Roundabouts, hockey rules—there's nothing a little explainer video can't do for us Nashvillians.

Games at super-loud Bridgestone Arena are a blast, often highlighted by chanting "You suck!" and "It's all your fault!" at the opposing team's goalie after a Predators goal. Additionally, fans enthusiastically shout "Thanks, Paul" to the team's PA announcer whenever he says one minute remains in the period. During the Stanley Cup playoffs, it's tradition to throw a catfish onto the ice, which one unlucky guy or gal smuggles into the arena by taping it to their bare chest.

Nashville Soccer Club (MLS)
A relatively new franchise in Nashville, the Nashville Soccer Club is perfect for the hip set who enjoy espresso and refer to soccer as "football." To the fan base's credit, led by their proverbial leader, Soccer Moses ("Let my people goal"), whenever our soccer team scores a goal, the celebrations at Geodis Park make the honky-tonks on Broadway seem tame by comparison.

Nashville Sounds (MiLB)

The Triple-A Sounds play at First Horizon Park, an excellent venue in which to grab a drink, play some mini golf, and not watch a lick of baseball. Indeed, attending a Sounds game is essentially an eating and drinking contest with a side of pitching. Still, it's a fun hangout for families and transplants alike, and not only do the Sounds have the best name in Nashville sports, they've also got the best uniforms. Special shout-out to the massive (142-foot-by-55-foot) guitar-shaped scoreboard, an homage to the original guitar-shaped scoreboard from the now-abandoned Greer Stadium near Fort Negley.

Vanderbilt Commodores (NCAA)

There are other collegiate teams in Nashville—Belmont, Lipscomb, TSU—but as a member of the Southeastern Conference (SEC), Vanderbilt has the most prominent school basketball team (and the SEC's least prominent football team). Before every home football game, a group or individual is selected to carry a giant gold anchor, a symbol of strength and support, from the locker room in McGugin Center to Vanderbilt Stadium and then "drop the anchor" at midfield to mark the start of the event. Who knows how a landlocked school got tapped with a sea captain for a mascot. We just know Commodore fans resemble drunk sailors who have perfected the art of tailgating.

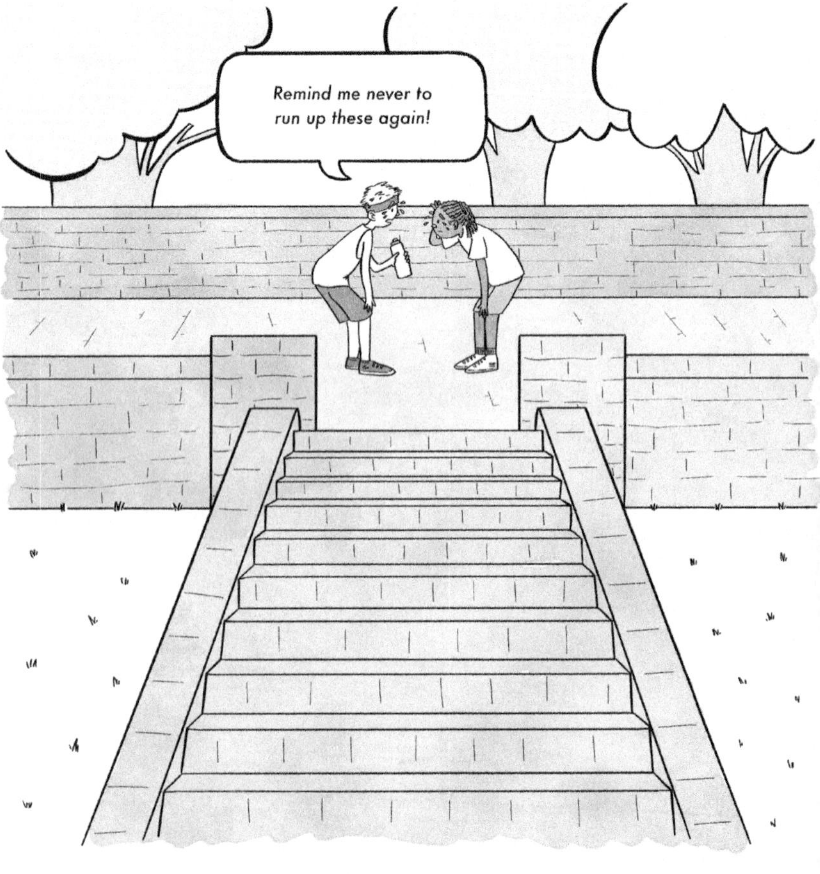
Remind me never to run up these again!

CHAPTER 12

Parks and Recreation

With all the eating and drinking there is to do in Nashville, it's not uncommon to see that your waistline has expanded. It's like the freshman fifteen in college. Don't worry, it happens to the best of us. And like any respectable city, Nashville offers plenty of green spaces to help you get back to your pre-South weight.

Centennial Park
Possibly the flagship of Nashville parks, this 132-acre space off West End Avenue offers a one-mile walking path, a man-made lake, and a full-scale replica of the Parthenon in Athens, Greece (although ours trumps that crumbling one they have over there). Originally built for Tennessee's 1897 Centennial Exposition as a temporary structure, the

Parthenon features a group of sixty-three paintings by nineteenth- and twentieth-century American artists, as well as a re-creation of the forty-two-foot statue of Athena, the largest indoor statue of its kind in the Western Hemisphere. When local sculptor Alan LeQuire sculpted the piece in 1990, he covered it in gold leaf and created a spear fashioned from an actual McDonald's flagpole.

Today, Centennial Park is where tourists will go to stare up at this statue and where you will go to sit on the Parthenon steps and watch a New Age fitness guy do his kettlebell routine. Feel free to join any number of soccer, volleyball, or Ultimate Frisbee games being played on the lawn, but please try to avoid the kettlebell guy.

> **Ultimate Frisbee**
> For those interested in ultimate, NightShade, our professional women's ultimate Frisbee team, whips through the air like ninja Frisbee warriors, unleashing a tornado of girl power on the field and proving that in Nashville, the only thing stronger than their throws is our love for unconventional sports.

The Warner Parks

Percy and Edwin Warner Parks, collectively referred to as "the Warner Parks," are comprised of more than 3,100 acres that include hiking trails, horse trails, dog parks, mountain biking courses, and a nature center. It is also the location of the Iroquois Steeplechase grounds and the gateway to the Cheekwood Estate and Gardens. At the main entrance to the Percy Warner Park section are the picturesque Allée steps, more commonly known as the Belle Meade Stairs, constructed in 1936 and renovated in 2020. Jogging up these steps serves as a reminder of how out of shape we all are. Something about the lack of give from the limestone makes it feel like a New York City walk-up that never ends. Better to do what everyone else does and stick to the ground level, where you can hire a photographer to take your family holiday or engagement photos.

Radnor Lake
Radnor Lake is like the Warner Parks' smaller, but no less refined, sister. The enjoyable Otter Creek Road Trail takes you around the perimeter of the placid lake, where wildlife enthusiasts have their best chance to observe owls, herons, and yes, even bald eagles. Astronomy lovers head for the hills of the Dyer Observatory, but again, please keep Bluebird on the Mountain a secret.

Shelby Park and Bottoms
Shelby is East Nashville's answer to the parks of its cross-river counterpart. Hugging the Cumberland River,

Shelby Bottoms has ten miles of paved walking and biking trails along with baseball fields, a nature center, and a disc golf course. For something a little different, head up to the northwest part of the park, where the abandoned Cornelia Fort Airpark allows for laps around a runway and a monthly pickin' party during the warmer months.

Sevier Park
Once a no-go zone for Nashville locals, Sevier Park has transformed into a lovely, leafy gathering space for hillside picnics, pickup tennis games, and low-key strolls away from the hustle and bustle of 12 South. Every Tuesday from May through October, the 12 South Farmers Market sets up shop on the south side of the park, offering local produce, live music, and a nice neighborhood ambiance.

Elmington Park
Why play tennis, softball, or pickup soccer when you can take part in Elmington Park's most famous pastime: medieval fantasy foam fighting. Every Sunday from noon until dark, grown adults clad in homemade armor whack each other with foam swords while pretending it's a legitimate sport. During this truly enchanting spectacle, Dur Demarion, the largest foam-fighting group in the South, conducts battle reenactments that would make George

R. R. Martin proud. For more information and the rules of battle, visit www.durdemarion.com. If live action role-playing, or "LARPing," isn't your speed, then check out Movies in the Park, Elmington's outdoor film series that takes place every Thursday throughout the summer.

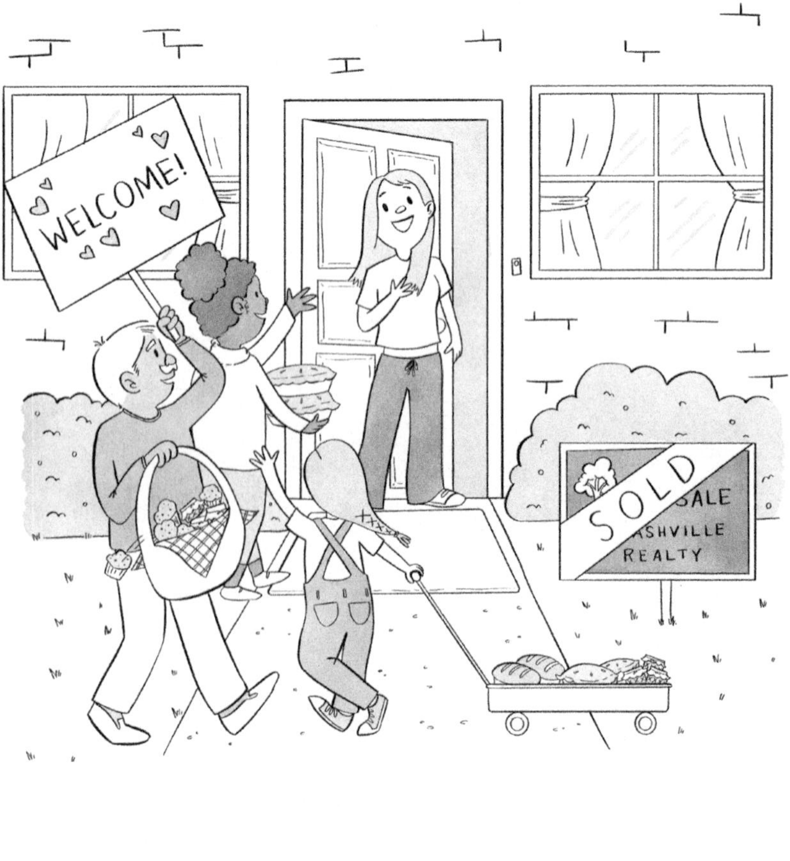
WELCOME!
SOLD
SALE
ASHVILLE
REALTY

CHAPTER 13

The Nashville Way

In 2016, *Travel + Leisure* magazine ranked Nashville as the friendliest city in America, prompting hordes of people to move to the Athens of the South.

However, locals worry the influx of newcomers may eventually compromise the warm and amiable nature of our cordial town. More than any new restaurant, music venue, or pretty park, it's the sense of community that makes this a desirable place to live (that and the lack of a state income tax). So here are a few simple things you can do to help keep Nashville friendly and warm.

Don't Be a Stranger
Maybe we've been watching too much Andy Griffith, but when you're out and about in the community, say

hello. Strike up a conversation. The Uber and Lyft drivers do it, so why not you?

Back in the neighborhood, you may find that when you first move into your new home, your neighbors will ring your doorbell with a plate of food or a casserole in hand to welcome you. Embrace them. Invite them in. Show them around. After all, you might just make a friend. Don't worry that they'll judge your new home. They've already seen it. Before you bought it, every neighbor took a tour when the real estate agent held the open house.

If a neighbor owns a dog that won't stop barking, don't report them to the homeowner's association or Nextdoor. That's what they do in California. Only outsiders start blowing petty nuisances out of proportion. Simply leave a note in their mailbox, wait until you casually bump into one another in the neighborhood, or knock on their door and talk with the person nicely. Here in Nashville, we prefer a good friendly chat over rules and regulations to help us solve the Case of the Noisy Lawn Mower or the Misplaced Garbage Cans. Call it Southern Conflict Resolution 101.

Embrace a Slower Pace
When waiting in line anywhere, but especially the pharmacy or grocery store, expect to find yourself in

a seemingly pointless conversation with the person in front of you, behind you, or both. Remember, they don't want anything but to pass the time with idle chitchat, make you laugh, and perhaps provide some needed encouragement. Lines tend to be long and slow because the checkout person may be showing customers pictures of their new grandchild or just feeling generally chatty about the weather. Slow down, take a deep breath, and accept the fact that you too will eventually get up to the cashier for your own lengthy exchange. The only time we're ever quiet in a group is during an in-the-round performance, because even the simplest errands can turn into a friendly encounter.

In Dolly We Trust

Perhaps we're so friendly because we're all just trying to do our best Dolly Parton impression. Dolly lives in Nashville, where she is revered as a national treasure, and no one embodies the giving spirit more than her. Her Imagination Library mails free books to children around the world from birth until age five, and in 2021 she donated $1 million to Vanderbilt University Medical Center to help Moderna develop the Covid vaccine. Don't mess with Dolly. Ever. We will ask you to leave town immediately. In fact, we'll happily drive you to the airport and put you on the next plane.

What to Do When You Suspect Ulterior Motives

Of course, you may have a hard time wrapping your head around our friendly nature. You might suspect some ulterior motive lurking behind our openness. We're not trying to steal your wallet, get your PIN, or abduct your dog. We're merely being neighborly. It helps pass the time, connects us with our fellow human beings, and makes life more interesting, because at the end of the day, we're all in this together. That said, if an unknown number calls offering cash for your home, hang up. Or rather, utilize the tools you've learned in this chapter by engaging in idle chitchat, making them laugh, and providing some needed encouragement until they forget why they originally called.

"...and one nation, under Dolly,
with liberty, and hot chicken for all."

CHAPTER 14

Nashville Citizenship Test

Congratulations! You've come a long way since the beginning of this book. Now that you've got the inside scoop, it's time to test your knowledge. Take this subjective and completely made-up Nashville citizenship test. If you pass, welcome to the club.

Nashville Citizenship Test
Ratified May 2024
Administered by the Music City Council of Elders
Enforced by Bart Durham Injury Law

Q: What is the name of the legislative authority that governs Nashville and Davidson County?
A: The Metropolitan Council, or "Metro."

Q: When was Nashville founded?
A: Christmas Eve 1779 by pioneer James Robertson.

Q: What is the state bird of Tennessee?
A: The construction crane. (We will also accept the hot chicken.)

Q: Why is Nashville called "Music City"?
A: Because in 1873, the Fisk Jubilee Singers were singing for Queen Victoria over in Europe, and she remarked, "My, you must be from a city of music." Which is much better than when they sang for Ulysses S. Grant at the White House, who remarked, "My, you must be from Middle Tennessee."

Q: Where does Dolly Parton sleep?
A: On her back.

Q: Complete this statement:
s. I believe in . . .
    a. Nashville.
s. Drive like your kids . . .
    a. live here.
s. It ain't the heat . . .
    a. it's the humidity.
s. These trendy new restaurants are great, but . . .
    a. nothing beats BrickTop's and Sperry's.

s. Pinewood Social is great, but . . .
　　a. nothing beats Tusculum Strike & Spare.
s. CycleBar is great, but . . .
　　a. nothing beats the Green Hills Y.

Q: How do you defuse a fight between Vanderbilt and Vols football fans?
A: By reminding them they both have to play Alabama and are screwed either way. (Other acceptable answers include replacing "Alabama" with: "Georgia," "Auburn," "Florida," or "the entire SEC.")

Q: Nashville is home to the largest community of which ethnic group in all of North America?
A: The Kurds.

Q: How do you pronounce Murfreesboro?
A: Exactly how it looks: Murfreerousborrowgghhh.

Q: How many murals does it take to attract a gaggle of bachelorettes?
A: Just one.

Q: You know you've become a Nashville local when . . .
A: Your eye begins to twitch the moment someone suggests, "Let's go out on Broadway!"

Q: Which four former US presidents have ties to Nashville?
A: Andrew Jackson, James K. Polk, Andrew Johnson, and, depending on how you feel about hanging chads, Al Gore.

Q: Who is Nashville's favorite superhero?
A: The Batman Building.

Excellent, you passed with flying colors. Now, if you really want to be considered a local, complete this handy checklist:

- ☐ **Eat at the Loveless Cafe.** Patiently wait in line for biscuits, country ham, and red-eye gravy so heavenly, it'll be one of your favorite Nashville meals.

- ☐ **Have a meal at Prince's Hot Chicken.** Test the limits of your spice tolerance, convince yourself that eating the extra-hot version is the equivalent of winning a fiery culinary marathon, and proudly display your "I survived Prince's" T-shirt like a badge of honor.

- ☐ **Dine at a meat & three.** Embark on a quest for the perfect balance between stuffing yourself like a Thanksgiving turkey and convincing yourself that the three side dishes make it a well-rounded, nutritious meal. Embrace the age-old dilemma of choosing between three delicious sides, only to end up ordering a fourth. It's the ultimate exercise in self-control as you attempt to resist ordering a second helping of mac and cheese.

- ☐ **Enjoy music at the Bluebird Cafe.** If you can get in, you'll hear some of the best songwriters in the country.

- ☐ **Enjoy music at the Station Inn.** This unassuming spot hosts the world's best bluegrass music seven nights a week.

- ☐ **Attend a show at the Ryman.** Enjoy unparalleled acoustics while sitting on church pews surrounded by stained glass.

- ☐ **Experience a show at the Ascend.** The Ascend is an open-air amphitheater located on the Cumberland River where you can hear a great show while enjoying local food and drinks in a relaxed atmosphere.

- ☐ **Visit the Rock Block.** At Nashville's counterculture epicenter on Elliston Place—home to Exit/In, the End, Samurai Sushi, and Elliston Place Soda Shop—the Rock Block is a magical barrier that keeps all the country music fans at bay, giving rock enthusiasts a haven to party.

- ☐ **Go to Bluebird on the Mountain.** This may be your only option for the iconic Bluebird experience, so brave the winding roads to witness a magical combination of talented songwriters and breathtaking views.

- ☐ **Hike Percy, Edwin, Radnor, and Shelby parks.** Spend a day experiencing each of these four incredible parks. Wonder. Wander. Repeat.

- ☐ **Volunteer for a day with Hands On Nashville.** Join forces with other Nashville locals, armed with enthusiasm and a questionable level of DIY skills, to tackle projects ranging from painting walls to planting gardens, all while secretly hoping you won't be responsible for any major disasters. It's a humbling experience that brings out the best in the community.

- ☐ **See each one of our sports teams play a game.** At a Titans, Predators, Soccer Club, or Sounds game, locals embrace the joy of collective victory or commiserate over defeat while bonding over the shared experience of cheering, chanting, and losing their voices in unison. It's a powerful reminder that in a city fueled by music, our sports teams provide a rhythmic heartbeat that unites us all, creating lasting memories and a sense of belonging that extends far beyond the final buzzer, whistle, or hot dog.

CHAPTER 14

- [ ] **Experience a summer outdoor movie at NightLight 615 or Movies in the Park.** Grab your lawn chair and head to NightLight 615 (at the Bicentennial Capitol Mall amphitheater) or Movies in the Park (at Elmington Park), where the warm breeze carries the aroma of barbecue and we all become amateur film critics, debating whether the movie or the food truck lineup really deserves the Oscar.

- [ ] **Enjoy music one spring or fall night at Musicians Corner at Centennial Park.** At this magical place where mosquitoes harmonize with guitars, finding a good spot on the lawn is a sport that only locals truly master. Come for the free music, stay for the sweat-soaked guitar solos, and leave with a newfound appreciation for the cooling powers of a well-timed snow cone.

- [ ] **Savor a cone at Bobbie's Dairy Dip.** The acclaimed Bobbie's Dairy Dip is an institution in Nashville serving burgers and soft-serve ice cream since 1951. There's always a line during the summer and hordes of people camped out at the outdoor tables.

- [ ] **Visit the Peach Truck.** The Peach Truck delivers handpicked, just-off-the-tree peaches from Georgia to booths and other locations across Nashville. Locals anxiously await their arrival each May.

- ☐ **Explore one of Nashville's farmers' markets.** Embrace your inner foodie and navigate through a maze of vegetable stands, locally raised meats, food trucks, and musicians.

- ☐ **Visit the zoo.** With more than 6,230 animals encompassing 339 species, the Nashville Zoo has a state-of-the-art tiger exhibit, an interactive Kangaroo Kickabout, and the largest Komodo dragon habitat in the Americas.

- ☐ **Visit Cheekwood, the Country Music Hall of Fame, the Frist Art Museum, the National Museum of African American Music, the Tennessee State Museum, and the Musicians Hall of Fame.** Explore the rich tapestry of art, history, and music in Nashville by spending an afternoon at each one of these fabulous museums.

- ☐ **Attend a show at the Schermerhorn Symphony Center.** At the Schermerhorn Symphony Center, immerse yourself in the mesmerizing world of the Grammy Award–winning Nashville Symphony.

- ☐ **Eat at the Blue Moon Waterfront Grille.** A laid-back waterfront dining destination on the Cumberland River.

CHAPTER 14

- ☐ **See the Time Jumpers at 3rd and Lindsley.** Legendary studio musicians come together most Monday nights to deliver a fantastic show, often joined by a surprise guest who'll knock your socks off. Just another typical night in Nashville, right?

- ☐ **Get lost in a book at Parnassus or McKay's.** Visit Nashville's hometown (and completely different!) bookstores in Green Hills and Bellevue, respectively.

Nashville Slang

across the river: East Nashville, the land that lies beyond the majestic Cumberland River, where many locals venture with a mixture of excitement and apprehension.

Athens of the South: A nickname for Nashville that Siri often confuses with cities named Athens in Georgia, Alabama, Mississippi, and Louisiana.

Batman Building: The AT&T Building, which resembles the Caped Crusader.

bless your heart: A charming Southern phrase delivered with faux politeness that leaves recipients wondering whether they've just been blessed or insulted.

BNA: The call sign for Nashville International Airport, and subsequently a nickname for the city. If you see someone wearing a "BNA" hat, that may be an indication they are "New Nashville" (see: New Nashville p. 125).

Buckle of the Bible Belt: You'll never find a city with more church signs offering divine wisdom, quirky puns, and occasional jokes than Nashville.

bus call: The time when musicians have to board the tour bus that will take them to a Waffle House or a Motel 6 on the road to their next gig.

Commodores: The nickname given to Vanderbilt University's athletic teams, in honor of the nickname given to founder Cornelius Vanderbilt, who had a successful career as a steamship entrepreneur but never actually held the official rank in the United States Navy.

East Nasty: The endearing nickname for East Nashville, a hip and edgy neighborhood.

fang fingers: The two-fingered hand gesture Nashville Predators fans make when an opposing team's player is headed to the penalty box.

fixin': The ultimate excuse for any unfinished or postponed task, allowing us to confidently declare, "I'm fixin' to do it," while secretly knowing that the job will probably remain on the back burner.

going to the 'Boro: Going to Murfreesboro, the largest suburb of Nashville, the sixth-largest city in the state, and the geographic center of Tennessee.

hold your horses: Pause for a moment before foolishly leaping into action, such as hopping aboard a mechanical bull after one too many shots of Jack Daniel's.

honky-tonkin': Hopping from one live music venue to the next along the Honky Tonk Highway, all while attempting to dodge pedal taverns in favor of pedal steel guitars.

hook-up: Nashville parents refer to the lane used to drop off and pick up their kids at school as the "hook-up line" or simply "hook-up." So, when school officials meet with you to discuss hook-up rules, rest assured there's no need to panic.

hose: We've shortened the word "hosepipe" to avoid an extra syllable and confuse out-of-state plumbers.

hot chicken: Our beloved local specialty that turns even the most stoic Nashvillians into sweating, fire-breathing dragons.

in-the-round: A captivating music performance where talented songwriters take turns sharing their original songs, creating an intimate and immersive experience for the audience.

It ain't the heat, it's the humidity: In Nashville, we blame the humidity for turning us into walking waterfalls.

Long Players: A group of highly skilled session musicians who occasionally pop up around town to perform a complete cover of an iconic album.

LOTG: Live on the Green, Nashville's free outdoor music festival sponsored by Lightning 100 and held in Public Square Park in early September.

meat & three: A diner or restaurant where you select your choice of meat and three sides (typically mashed potatoes, baked beans, corn, and collard greens).

Mother Church: Ryman Auditorium, Nashville's most beloved concert venue, originally a church.

NashVegas: A self-deprecating nickname for Music City due to Broadway's kitschy similarity to Sin City.

New Nashville: Nashville post ~2010. Depending on who you ask, it is either a pejorative term to describe a Nashville that has lost its way with its experience-driven traps and celebrity-backed bars, or a symbol of the city's economic growth and cultural prowess.

Old Nashville: Nashville pre ~2010. Depending on who you ask, it is either a romanticized term to describe the preservation of what made Nashville cool, like the Ryman Auditorium and Robert's Western World, or a cautionary reference to when Broadway was seedy and Nashville was dead.

pickin' party: A potluck, but instead of bringing casseroles, guests show up with their guitars, banjos, and fiddles, and sing their hearts out.

Predneck: A fan of the Nashville Predators hockey team.

Preds: The nickname of Nashville's professional hockey team.

Recession Special: The most famous menu item at Robert's Western World: a fried bologna sandwich, chips, Moon Pie, and PBR for only $6.

SATCo: The San Antonio Taco Company, the popular Tex-Mex eatery founded in 1984 near Vanderbilt University that makes everything fresh from scratch daily.

scattered, smothered, covered, and chunked: In Waffle House parlance, having your hash browns crisped, smothered in sauteed onions, covered in melted American cheese, and sprinkled with diced ham. Also, how some people end up after a bad night on Broadway.

Smashville: The electrifying nickname that encapsulates the wild energy of Nashville's hockey scene, where the thunderous roar of the crowd, crashing bodies, and slap shots rival a country rock concert.

Southern charm: Sweet politeness sometimes laced with a dash of backhanded compliments that fly under the radar.

stompin' grounds: Where wannabe cowboys and cowgirls wear oversized hats while sipping on fancy cocktails in rooftop bars.

supper: A fancy Southern way of saying "dinner" to make a regular meal sound like a sophisticated event.

Swarmageddon: The cyclical invasion of billions of noisy cicadas emerging from the ground every thirteen and seventeen years, creating a deafening and horrific natural spectacle.

tall and skinny: The term for impossibly lean houses miraculously squeezed onto a tiny plot of land.

tax-free weekend: Tennessee's annual holiday when we race out to purchase school supplies, clothing, and computers without having to pay the 9.25 percent sales tax, convinced we're somehow outsmarting the system.

"Thanks, Paul": What Nashville Predators fans shout when the team's PA announcer, Paul McCann, announces there is one minute remaining in the period.

Titans: Our cardiac arrest-inducing football team, which, season after season, finds new and inventive ways to snatch defeat from the jaws of victory.

T-Rac: The official mascot of the Tennessee Titans, a raccoon who rides a four-wheeler during breaks.

unicorn: A parking spot downtown on a Saturday night, an affordable apartment in the heart of the city, or a live music venue not inundated with bachelorette parties, because just like a mythical creature, you can search high and low for it, but the chances of actually finding one are about as good as the chances of winning the lottery.

Vandy Boys: An endearing nickname for baseball players at Vanderbilt University.

Vols: Short for "Volunteers," it's the affectionate nickname of the University of Tennessee sports teams, whose die-hard fans proudly sport orange-and-white clothing and painted faces.

woo girl: The nickname for a bachelorette, referred to as such for the loud "WOOOOO!" sound she makes while gallivanting around Nashville.

y'all: A useful word you will come to use habitually (don't try to fight it), created by contracting the words "you" and "all."

Bibliography

"411 Broadway Sold" by Meg Wrather, *Nashville Business Journal*, January 3, 2022, www.bizjournals.com/nashville/news/2022/01/03/411-broadway-sold.html.

"Arrival of the Mud-Covered Man Started Country Music" by Bill Carey, *Tennessee Magazine*, www.tnmagazine.org/arrival-of-the-mud-covered-man-started-country-music/.

"British Airways Bringing Nashville and London Closer with New Direct Flight and Fisk Jubilee Singers" by Julie Thanki, *Tennessean*, www.tennessean.com/story/entertainment/music/2018/05/04/british-airways-nashville-london-flight-fisk-jubilee-singers/581611002/.

"The Civil War's Impact on Prostitution in Nashville" by Erin Blakemore, History.com, www.history.com/news/civil-war-prostitution-nashville.

"Country Music's Culture Wars and the Remaking of Nashville" by Emily Nussbaum, *New Yorker*, July 24, 2023, www.newyorker.com/magazine/2023/07/24/country-musics-culture-wars-and-the-remaking-of-nashville.

"Dutchmen's Curve Train Wreck" by Kevin Hoch, Historical Marker Database, February 13, 2012, revised February 7, 2023, www.hmdb.org/m.asp?m=52596.

"Exclusive: Saber-tooth Bones Named for Preds Get New Home at Bridgestone

Arena" by Jessica Bliss, *Tennessean*, November 6, 2016, www.tennessean.com/story/news/2016/11/06/exclusive-saber-tooth-bones-named-preds-get-new-home-bridgestone-arena/92829882/.

Fodor's Inside Nashville by Brittney McKenna (New York, New York: Fodor's Travel, 2019).

"From Hockey 101 in Nashville to a PhD with Predators" by Ben Shpigel, New York Times, May 22, 2017, www.nytimes.com/2017/05/22/sports/hockey/from-hockey-101-in-nashville-to-a-phd-with-predators.html.

"George D. Hay," Country Music Hall of Fame and Museum, www.countrymusichalloffame.org/hall-of-fame/george-d-hay.

"Health Care Industry Economic Impact," Nashville Health Care Council, https://healthcarecouncil.com/health-care-industry/economic-impact/.

"Infrastructure," Nashville Area Chamber of Commerce, www.nashvillechamber.com/economic-development/relocate-or-expand/infrastructure.

"In the Heart of Nashville, Rolling Parties Rage at Every Stoplight" by Rick Rojas, *New York Times*, September 19, 2021.

Moon 52 Things to Do in Nashville by Margaret Littman (Berkeley, CA: Avalon Travel, 2022).

"Music Row on This Year's 11 Most Endangered," National Trust for Historic Preservation, savingplaces.org/places/nashvilles-music-row/updates/music-row-on-this-years-11-most-endangered.

"Nashville: Athens of the South . . . but Why?" by Sarah Arntz, Nashville Public Library Blog, library.nashville.org/blog/2019/10/nashville-athens-southbut-why.

Nashville Bachelorettes: A Ben Oddo Investigation, directed by Rachel Neubeck, performance by Ben Oddo (MFIC Entertainment, 2023).

"Nashville Flood: 20 Things to Know" by Karen Grigsby, *Tennessean*, April 30, 2015, www.tennessean.com/story/news/local/2015/04/30/nashville-flood-20-things-to-know/26653901/

Nashville Like a Local: By the People Who Call It Home by Bailey Freeman and Kristen Shoates (New York: DK Publishing, 2022).

Nashville Songwriter: The Inside Stories Behind Country Music's Greatest Hits by Jake Brown (Dallas: Ben Bella Books, 2014).

"NFL Player's Incredible Beer Run in Nashville" by Chris Strauss, *USA Today*, November 6, 2012, www.usatoday.com/story/gameon/2012/11/06/nfl-bears-beer-nashville/1685913/.

"Nunbun," Bongo Roasting Co., www.bongojava.com/pages/nunbun.

Parks: A Guide to Nashville's Neighborhoods (Nashville: Parks Real Estate, 2022).

"Railroads Turned Tennessee Towns into Cities" by Bill Carey, Tennessee Magazine, www.tnmagazine.org/railroads-turned-tennessee-towns-into-cities/.

"Romance of Nashville Mayor Is the Talk of the Town: Politics: Bill Boner is engaged although he is still married to his third wife. The couple's very public romance has both angered and amused residents" by Lee May, *Los Angeles Times*, August 16, 1990, www.latimes.com/archives/la-xpm-1990-08-16-mn-1041-story.html.

"The Story of Music City," Visit Music City, www.visitmusiccity.com/explore-nashville/music/story-music-city.

"Why Half of Nashville's Roads Still Don't Have Sidewalks" by Rachel Martin, Bloomberg, January 6, 2017, www.bloomberg.com/news/articles/2017-01-06/why-half-of-nashville-s-roads-still-don-t-have-sidewalks.

Acknowledgments

Thanks to Nick Spiva, Steve Dennison, Amy Dennison, Jacqueline Ruger Hutton, Will Spiva, Shane Tallant, Brian Stoltzvus, Axson West, Will Robinson, Bill Seymour, and Ben Oddo for their insights.

About the Author

Michelle Spiva, a lifelong Southerner, has lived in Nashville for more than thirty years. A graduate of Vanderbilt University, where she earned her bachelor's degree and law degree, she subsequently practiced law for twenty years. Michelle and her husband enjoy building and remodeling houses and investing in commercial real estate. When not working, she enjoys spending time with her family, traveling, playing pickleball, and hiking.

A portion of the proceeds from the sale of each copy of this book will be donated to the Nashville Musicians Association Crisis Assistance Fund.

Printed in Great Britain
by Amazon